low-carb

breakfast & brunch • appetizers & snacks
soups & salads • seafood & meat • vegetarian dishes
• desserts

mc
raé
PUBLISHING

This book was conceived, edited and designed by McRae Publishing Ltd London

Copyright © 2012 McRae Publishing Ltd

www.mcraebooks.com

NOTE TO OUR READERS
Eating eggs or egg whites that are not completely cooked poses the possibility of salmonella food poisoning. The risk is greater for pregnant women, the elderly, the very young, and persons with impaired immune systems. If you are concerned about salmonella, you can use reconstituted powdered egg whites or pasteurized eggs.

Culinary Notebooks series

Project Director Anne McRae
Art Director Marco Nardi

LOW-CARB
Photography Brent Parker Jones
Text Carla Bardi
Nutritionist Penny Doyle
Editing Helen Cartwright, Daphne Trotter
Food Styling Lee Blaylock
Food Styling Assistant Rochelle Seator
Prop Styling Lee Blaylock
Layouts Aurora Granata
Prepress Filippo Delle Monache

ISBN 978-88-6098-350-3

Printed in China

contents

getting started

There are 100 delicious low-carb recipes in this book. The amount of carbohydrates in each serving is given in the green circle next to each recipe. Most of the recipes are simple and quick to prepare. They are all rated for difficulty: 1 (simple), 2 (fairly simple), or 3 (challenging). In these two pages we have highlighted 25 of the most enticing recipes, just to get you started!

 SIMPLE

GRILLED VEGGIE platter

SPICY stuffed eggs

TUNA pâté

BANANA SPICE cake

BEEF stew

BABY frittatas

CELERY & CHEESE snacks

 QUICK

CHICKEN salad

BEEF & LETTUCE cups

BERRY FRUIT salad

CLASSICS

MELON & PROSCIUTTO medley

SCOTCH eggs

COCK-A-LEEKIE
soup

SEAFOOD salad

SOUVLAKI

SPICY EGGS
with tomatoes

BROCCOLI SOUP
with stilton

EDITOR'S CHOICE

INDONESIAN
beef satay

ALMOND
cookies

TEX-MEX chili soup

| BEST BREAKFAST | BEST SOUP | BEST SALAD | BEST MEAT DISH | BEST DESSERT |

NUT & SEED
granola

BEEF & VEGGIE
soup

STEAK SALAD
with papaya

ZUCCHINI
lasagna

CITRUS
pound cake

breakfast & brunch

NUT & SEED granola

1 cup (120 g) sunflower seeds
1 cup (150 g) unsweetened shredded (desiccated) coconut
1 cup (120 g) pecans, coarsely chopped
1 cup (120 g) walnuts, coarsely chopped
1 cup (120 g) almonds, coarsely chopped
$^1/_2$ cup (60 g) flaxseeds
$^1/_2$ cup (75 g) wheat bran
$^1/_3$ cup (90 ml) rice bran oil
2 teaspoons ground cinnamon
1 teaspoon vanilla extract (essence)

CARBS 6g

Serves 12 • Preparation 10 minutes • Cooking 25–30 minutes Difficulty 1

1. Preheat the oven to 325°F (170°C/gas 3).

2. Mix the sunflower seeds, coconut, pecans, walnuts, almonds, flaxseeds, and wheat bran in a large roasting pan. Drizzle with the oil. Stir in the cinnamon and vanilla.

3. Toast in the oven for 25–30 minutes, stirring every 10 minutes. The granola should be toasted and pale golden brown when ready.

4. Let cool to room temperature. Pack into an airtight container so that the granola stays crisp.

If you liked this recipe, you will love these as well.

CITRUS pound cake

BANANA SPICE cake

ALMOND cookies

Eggs are the perfect low-carb food. Packed with essential vitamins and minerals, and a very good source of low-cost protein, they contain very few carbohydrates. Serve a platter of these warm baby frittatas for a casual breakfast or brunch with family and friends.

BABY frittatas

8	large eggs
1/2	cup (120 ml) whole milk
1/2	teaspoon freshly ground black pepper
1/4	teaspoon salt
4	ounces (120 g) thinly sliced prosciutto (parma ham), chopped
1/3	cup (40 g) freshly grated Parmesan cheese
2	tablespoons finely chopped fresh parsley

CARBS
4g

Serves 4 • Preparation 15 minutes • Cooking 8–10 minutes
Difficulty 1

1. Preheat the oven to 375°F (190°C/gas 5). Spray two 24-cup mini muffin pans with nonstick spray.

2. Whisk the eggs, milk, pepper, and salt in a large bowl until well blended. Stir in the prosciutto, Parmesan, and parsley. Fill the muffin cups almost to the top with the egg mixture.

3. Bake for 8–10 minutes, until the egg mixture is puffed and set in the center.

4. Use a rubber spatula to loosen the baby frittatas from the muffin cups and slide them onto a serving platter. Serve warm.

If you liked this recipe, you will love these as well.

FRENCH omelet

BOILED EGGS
& sausage stew

EGG & CHORIZO
cocottes

FRENCH omelet

 Serves 2 • Preparation 10 minutes • Cooking 5 minutes • Difficulty 1

5	large eggs		Salt and freshly ground black pepper
1	tablespoon finely chopped fresh parsley	2	tablespoons butter
1	tablespoon finely chopped fresh chives		Sprigs of fresh parsley, to garnish
1	tablespoon finely chopped fresh tarragon		

1. Beat the eggs, parsley, chives, and tarragon in a large bowl. Season with salt and pepper.

2. Melt the butter in a small frying pan over medium heat. Pour in the beaten eggs. When the bottom has set, slide a wooden spatula under the eggs to loosen them from the pan. Shake the pan with a rotating movement. Cook until nicely browned on the underside. Tilt the pan away from the handle and, using a spatula, fold over two sides into the center.

3. Slide a spatula under the omelet and slide it onto a serving plate. Garnish with the sprigs of parsley. Serve hot.

SPICY EGGS with tomatoes

 Serves 4 • Preparation 5 minutes • Cooking 5 minutes • Difficulty 1

8	large eggs	1¹/₂	cups (75 g) fresh cilantro (coriander) leaves
1	cup (250 ml) heavy (double) cream		
4	large tomatoes, cut into small cubes	¹/₃	cup (90 ml) Thai sweet chili sauce

1. Beat the eggs and cream in a large bowl.

2. Cook the egg mixture in a large nonstick frying pan over medium-low heat for about 5 minutes, stirring often, until the eggs form large chunks.

3. Serve the scrambled eggs hot with the tomatoes, cilantro, and sweet chili sauce.

BOILED EGGS & sausage stew

 Serves 4 • Preparation 10 minutes • Cooking 20–25 minutes • Difficulty 1

1	onion, finely chopped	1	(14-ounce/400-g) can tomatoes, with juice
4	pork sausages, coarsely chopped		
2	tablespoons extra-virgin olive oil	4	large eggs

1. Cook the onion and sausage in the oil in a large frying pan over medium-low heat until beginning to brown, about 5 minutes.

2. Add the tomatoes. Simmer until thickened and reduced, 10–15 minutes.

3. Meanwhile, cook the eggs in a medium saucepan of barely simmering water for 7 minutes. Drain well.

4. Place the eggs in eggcups and cut off the tops. Serve the sausage ragout hot with the eggs.

EGG & CHORIZO cocottes

Serves 4 • Preparation 10 minutes • Cooking 25–30 minutes • Difficulty 1

3	tablespoons butter	¹/₂	cup (125 ml) heavy (double) cream
8	ounces (250 g) Spanish chorizo sausage, cut into small cubes		
2	small leeks, trimmed and finely sliced	4	large eggs

1. Preheat the oven to 375°F (190°C/gas 5). Grease four ramekins with 1 tablespoon of the butter.

2. Melt the remaining 2 tablespoons of butter in a large frying pan. Add the chorizo and sauté for 3 minutes over medium heat.

3. Add the leeks and sauté for 3 minutes. Pour in the cream and cook over low heat for about 2 minutes, until the cream has thickened slightly.

4. Arrange the ramekins in a deep baking pan and pour in the mixture. Break an egg into the center of each ramekin. Fill the baking pan with boiling water to come halfway up the sides of the ramekins.

5. Bake for 15–18 minutes, until the eggs have set. Serve hot.

Traditional hash browns are made with potatoes and eggs. In this low-carb version, we have replaced the potatoes with coarsely grated zucchini. Not only are zucchini a good low-carb vegetable option, but they are also a good source of vitamins C, B6, and riboflavin.

ZUCCHINI hash browns

2   cups (400 g) coarsely grated zucchini (courgettes)

4   large eggs, beaten

1   small white onion, finely chopped

1   clove garlic, finely chopped

1   tablespoon finely chopped fresh parsley

    Salt and freshly ground black pepper

2   tablespoons extra-virgin olive oil

    Tomato ketchup, to serve

 Serves 2 • Preparation 15 minutes • Cooking 20 minutes • Difficulty 1

1. Combine the zucchini, eggs, onion, garlic, and parsley in a large bowl. Season with salt and pepper and mix well.

2. Heat 1 tablespoon of oil in a large frying pan over medium-high heat. Add half the zucchini mixture, spreading it to an even depth. Cook until browned, then flip and cook the other side, about 5 minutes each side.

3. Slice onto a plate. Cook the remaining zucchini mixture in the same way.

4. Serve warm, with the ketchup.

If you liked this recipe, you will love these as well.

BABY fritattas

SPICY EGGS
with tomatoes

SPINACH & CHEESE
tarts

SPINACH & CHEESE tarts

12 ounces (350 g) frozen chopped spinach

1 bunch scallions (spring onions), white part only, finely chopped

4 large eggs, lightly beaten

16 ounces (450 g) cottage cheese

2 cups (250 g) coarsely grated Cheddar cheese

1 cup (50 g) mixed baby salad greens, to serve

 Serves 4 • Preparation 10 minutes • Cooking 50–60 minutes Difficulty 1

1. Preheat the oven to 325°F (170°C/gas 3). Lightly grease four 4-inch (10-cm) tartlet pans.

2. Put the spinach in a small saucepan with 1 cup (250 ml) of water. Cook over medium heat, stirring occasionally, until tender, 3–5 minutes. Drain well, squeezing out excess moisture with your hands. Place in a bowl and stir in the scallions, eggs, and both cheeses. Divide the mixture evenly among the prepared pans.

3. Bake for 45–55 minutes, until the eggs are set. Serve warm with the salad greens.

ALMOND pancakes

2   large eggs, separated
1   cup (120 g) finely ground almonds (almond meal)
3   teaspoons sugar
4   tablespoons (60 g) butter, softened
¼   teaspoon salt
1   tablespoon mild-flavored olive oil
¼   cup (60 ml) water

 CARBS 4g

Serves 6 • Preparation 15 minutes • Cooking 8–12 minutes
Difficulty 1

1. Put the egg whites in a big bowl and the egg yolks in a small bowl.

2. Add the almond meal, sugar, 2 tablespoons of butter, salt, oil, and water to the bowl with the egg yolks and mix well.

3. Beat the egg whites until soft peaks form. Fold the almond mixture into the egg whites as gently as possible.

4. Heat 1 tablespoon of the remaining butter in a large frying pan. Drop tablespoons of the batter into the pan and cook until golden brown, 2–3 minutes. Turn and cook on the other side. Repeat with the remaining butter and batter. Serve warm.

appetizers & snacks

TUNA pâté

2   tablespoons butter
2   cloves garlic, finely chopped
1   small onion, finely chopped
8   ounces (250 g) cream cheese
1   (6-ounce/180-g) can tuna, drained
1   tablespoon freshly squeezed orange juice
1   tablespoon finely grated unwaxed orange zest
1   tablespoon finely chopped fresh parsley
     Salt and freshly ground black pepper
     Thin slices of scallion (spring onions), to serve (optional)
     Celery sticks, to serve
     Carrot sticks, to serve

CARBS 2g • Serves 6 • Preparation 10 minutes + 1–2 hours to chill • Cooking 3–4 minutes • Difficulty 1

1. Heat the butter in a small frying pan over medium heat. Add the garlic and onion and sauté until softened, 3–4 minutes. Set aside to cool a little.

2. Combine the cream cheese, tuna, orange juice, orange zest, and parsley in a food processor. Season with salt and pepper. Chop until blended. Add the cooled onion mixture and chop until smooth.

3. Spoon the pâté into a bowl. Cover with plastic wrap (cling film) and chill in the refrigerator for 1–2 hours before serving. Garnish with slices of scallion, if liked, and serve with the carrot and celery sticks.

If you liked this recipe, you will love these as well.

SMOKED SALMON dip

SPINACH & SALMON pâté

PLOWMAN'S pâté

This is an old-fashioned appetizer that has never really gone out of style. If you don't like spicy food, don't add the chili powder. To vary the flavor, replace the chili powder with curry powder.

SPICY stuffed eggs

6 large eggs
2 tablespoons mayonnaise
1 clove garlic, minced
2 teaspoons cider vinegar
1 tablespoon finely chopped cilantro (coriander) + extra leaves, to garnish
1/2 teaspoon hot chili powder
   Salt and freshly ground black pepper

CARBS 0g

Serves 6 • Preparation 10 minutes • Cooking 7–8 minutes
Difficulty 1

1. Boil the eggs until just firm, 7–8 minutes. Let cool a little then peel and cut in half lengthwise.

2. Use a teaspoon to carefully scoop out the yolks. Place the yolks in a small bowl and add the mayonnaise, garlic, cider vinegar, cilantro, and chili powder. Season with salt and pepper and mash with a fork until smooth.

3. Use the teaspoon to return the yolk mixture to the hollow egg whites. Garnish with the extra cilantro and serve.

If you liked this recipe, you will love these as well.

8

BABY fritattas

14

SPINACH & CHEESE tarts

20

SCOTCH eggs

SALMON cakes

CARBS 6g · Serves 4 • Preparation 10 minutes • Cooking 10–15 minutes • Difficulty 1

1 pound (500 g) salmon fillets, skin and bones removed
2 large egg whites, lightly beaten
3 tablespoons finely chopped fresh cilantro (coriander)

1 cup (250 ml) canola oil
1/2 cup (120 ml) Thai sweet chili sauce

1. Finely dice the salmon and transfer to a medium bowl. Add the egg whites and cilantro and stir to combine well.

2. Heat the oil in a large frying pan over medium-high heat. Place 2 tablespoons of the salmon mixture in the oil and fry until light golden, 1–2 minutes on each side. Repeat with the remaining salmon mixture. Place the salmon cakes on paper towels to drain off any excess oil.

3. Serve hot with the chili sauce for dipping.

SMOKED SALMON dip

CARBS 0.3g · Serves 4 • Preparation 10 minutes + 1 hour to chill · Difficulty 1

5 ounces (150 g) smoked salmon
8 ounces (250 g) cream cheese, at room temperature
2 tablespoons freshly squeezed lemon juice
1 1/2 tablespoons salt-cured capers, rinsed

2 tablespoons finely chopped fresh dill + an extra sprig, to garnish
Freshly ground black pepper
Carrot sticks, to serve
Celery sticks, to serve

1. Process the smoked salmon, cream cheese, lemon juice, capers, and dill in a food processor until smooth. Season with pepper.

2. Spoon the dip into a serving bowl. Cover with plastic wrap (cling film) and chill for at least an hour.

3. Garnish with the extra dill, and serve with the carrot and celery sticks.

SCOTCH eggs

CARBS 16g · Serves 8 • Preparation 20 minutes • Cooking 5–7 minutes • Difficulty 2

1 1/2 pounds (750 g) sausage meat
1 cup (250 ml) tomato salsa or chutney
8 hard-boiled eggs, peeled

1 cup (150 g) finely ground almonds
4 cups (1 liter) canola oil, for deep frying

1. Mix the sausage meat and 1/3 cup (90 ml) of the tomato chutney in a large bowl. Divide the sausage mixture into eight portions. Use your hands to form the sausage mixture around the hard-boiled eggs. Roll in the almonds until well-coated.

2. Heat the oil in a large, deep frying pan. Fry the eggs in batches for 5–7 minutes, until golden brown all over. Drain on paper towels.

3. Serve hot or at room temperature with the remaining tomato chutney.

SCRAMBLED EGGS & salmon

CARBS 1g · Serves 4 • Preparation 5 minutes • Cooking 5 minutes · Difficulty 1

8 large eggs
1 cup (250 ml) heavy (double) cream
1/4 cup (60 g) butter, cut up

8 slices smoked salmon
3 cups (150 g) arugula (rocket)

1. Beat the eggs and cream in a large bowl.

2. Melt the butter in a large frying pan over medium-low heat. Add the egg mixture and cook, stirring often, until the eggs form large chunks, about 5 minutes.

3. Serve the scrambled eggs hot with the smoked salmon and arugula.

SALMON CARPACCIO with lemon & thyme

1	teaspoon coarse sea salt
2	tablespoons brine-cured green peppercorns, drained
1–2	teaspoons fresh thyme leaves
$\frac{1}{2}$	cup (120 ml) extra-virgin olive oil
	Freshly squeezed juice of 1 lemon
1	pound (500 g) very fresh salmon fillet, thinly sliced
1	lemon, cut into wedges, to garnish

 CARBS 0g · Serves 6 • Preparation 15 minutes + 4 hours to chill • Difficulty 1

1. Coarsely pound the salt and half the peppercorns using a mortar and pestle. Add the thyme and mix well.

2. Whisk $\frac{1}{3}$ cup (90 ml) of the oil with the lemon juice and salt mixture in a small bowl.

3. Arrange the salmon on a large serving dish and pour the dressing over the top. Cover with plastic wrap (cling film) and chill in the refrigerator for 4 hours.

4. Remove the plastic wrap and drizzle with the remaining oil. Garnish with the remaining peppercorns and the lemon wedges and serve.

CELERY & CHEESE snacks

8   ounces (250 g) fresh ricotta
     cheese, drained
4   ounces (120 g) blue cheese,
     crumbled into small pieces
1/4 cup (60 ml) whole milk
1–2 cloves garlic, finely chopped
1   tablespoon finely chopped
     fresh chives
1   tablespoon extra-virgin
     olive oil
     Salt and freshly ground black
     pepper
10   large stalks very fresh celery
1   tablespoon finely chopped
     fresh parsley

 CARBS 3g

Serves 4 • Preparation 15 minutes + 1 hour to chill • Difficulty 1

1. Put the ricotta in a bowl. Add the blue cheese and milk and mash until smooth and creamy. Add the garlic, chives, oil, salt, and pepper, mixing well.

2. Cover with plastic wrap (cling film) and chill in the refrigerator for 1 hour.

3. Trim the celery stalks and remove any tough external fibers. Cut into pieces about 3 inches (8 cm) long.

4. Fill the celery with the cheese mixture, sprinkle with the parsley, and serve.

This is another classic appetizer that you may not think of as low-carb. Serve as an appetizer before a fish or meat main course or as a healthy snack.

MELON & PROSCIUTTO medley

1	medium cantaloupe (rock) melon
12	large, paper thin slices best-quality Italian prosciutto

 CARBS 6g Serves 6 • Preparation 10 minutes • Difficulty 1

1. Cut the melon in half and remove the seeds and pith. Slice into quarters and then slice each quarter into three. You will have 12 wedges. Remove the skin from each wedge then put the wedges back into their skins.

2. Arrange the melon wedges in their skins on a large serving platter. Drape the slices of prosciutto over the melon decoratively and serve.

If you liked this recipe, you will love these as well.

CELERY & CHEESE
snacks

WINTER
salad

ORANGE & ARTICHOKE
salad

SPINACH & SALMON pâté

Pâté

14 ounces (400 g) fresh salmon

3 large eggs

Salt and freshly ground black pepper

Pinch of freshly grated nutmeg

14 ounces (400 g) fresh spinach leaves, chopped

²/₃ cup (150 ml) heavy (double) cream

Sauce

¹/₃ cup (100 g) blackcurrant preserves (jam)

Zest of ¹/₂ unwaxed orange, in one long piece, removed with a sharp knife

Freshly squeezed juice of 1 orange

1 teaspoon white wine vinegar

 CARBS 7g Serves 6 • Preparation 20 minutes + 12 hours to chill • Cooking: 65 minutes • Difficulty 1

Pâté

1. Preheat the oven to 350°F (180°C/gas 4). Butter a 5 x 9-inch (13 x 23-cm) loaf pan. Wrap the outside with aluminum foil to make waterproof.

2. Cut 5 ounces (150 g) of the salmon into small cubes. Chop the remaining salmon coarsely. Process the eggs and coarsely chopped salmon in a food processor. Season with salt and pepper. Add the nutmeg and blend to make a smooth paste. Add the spinach a little at a time, chopping until smooth. Stir in the cream and salmon cubes by hand.

3. Spoon the mixture into the prepared pan. Cover with aluminum foil. Place the pan in a baking pan half-filled with water. Bake until set, about 1 hour. Let cool. Chill overnight.

Sauce

1. Bring the preserves, orange zest, orange juice, and vinegar to a boil over low heat. Simmer for 2–3 minutes. Discard the orange zest.

2. Turn the pâté out onto a serving dish. Slice thickly and serve with sauce spooned over the top.

PLOWMAN'S pâté

1 pound (500 g) pork loin, coarsely chopped

14 ounces (400 g) pig liver, coarsely chopped

8 ounces (250 g) lard or bacon fat, coarsely chopped

1 large onion, finely chopped

1 clove garlic, finely chopped

1 tablespoon green pepper-corns preserved in brine, rinsed and drained

12 black peppercorns

1/4 teaspoon grated nutmeg
Salt

1/3 cup (90 ml) Calvados (apple brandy)

2 bay leaves

4 cloves

1 1/2 cups (375 ml) water

1 tablespoon powdered gelatin
Pickled vegetables, to garnish
Fresh parsley, to garnish

 CARBS 6g • Serves 8 • Preparation 20 minutes + 24 hours to chill • Cooking 90 minutes • Difficulty 3

1. Preheat the oven to 350°F (180°C/gas 4). Oil a 5 x 9-inch (13 x 23-cm) loaf pan.

2. Place the pork loin and liver in a large bowl. Add the lard, onion, garlic, green peppercorns, black peppercorns, nutmeg, and salt. Stir in the Calvados. Transfer the mixture to the prepared pan and smooth the surface using the back of a spoon. Top with the bay leaves and cloves.

3. Bake until cooked through and lightly browned, about 90 minutes. Remove from the oven and drain the juices into a large saucepan. Skim off and discard any fat. Let cool.

4. Put the water in the saucepan. Add the gelatin and mix well. Bring to a boil over low heat, stirring until the gelatin has completely dissolved. Set aside to cool.

5. Pour the gelatin mixture over the pâté. Cover and chill for 24 hours. Turn the pâté out onto a serving dish. Slice and serve with the pickled vegetables and parsley.

Ceviche comes from the coastal regions of Mexico and other Latin American countries. It is based on uncooked fish, although you can't really say that the dish is raw, because the fish is marinated in lemon or lime juice which "cooks" the flesh.

CEVICHE

1	pound (500 g) very fresh red snapper or sea bass filets, cut into 1/2-inch (1-cm) cubes
1/2	cup (120 ml) freshly squeezed lemon juice
1	small red onion, minced
1/2	cup (120 ml) freshly squeezed lime juice
1	teaspoon salt
1	large stalk celery, diced
1	fresh jalapeno pepper, seeds removed, minced
1	fresh pimento pepper, seeds removed, minced
1/2	cup finely diced red bell pepper
2	ripe tomatoes, seeded and diced
2	tablespoons finely chopped fresh parsley
1/2	cup chopped fresh cilantro (coriander) + extra, to garnish
1/4	teaspoon fresh black pepper
2	ripe avocados, peeled, pitted, and cut into strips

CARBS 5g Serves 6 • Preparation 15 minutes + 4 hours to marinate
Difficulty 1

1. Marinate the fish and lemon juice in a large glass bowl for 3 hours. The fish will turn white.

2. Marinate the onion with the lime juice and salt in a separate bowl for 15 minutes. Add the celery, jalapeno, pimento, and bell pepper and let sit 15 minutes more.

3. Drain the fish in a colander. Rinse carefully with cold water. Drain well. Add the fish to the lime and onion mixture. Stir in the tomatoes, parsley, cilantro, and black pepper. Let the mixture sit for 30 minutes to allow the flavors to develop.

4. Use glass serving dishes or shrimp cocktail glasses. Spoon some of the ceviche into the bottom of each glass, top with avocado, layer with more ceviche, then more avocado and ceviche. Garnish with extra cilantro and lime, and serve.

If you liked this recipe, you will love these as well.

TUNA pâté

SALMON CARPACCIO
with lemon & thyme

NIÇOISE salad

ZUCCHINI soufflés

2 tablespoons extra-virgin olive oil
1 clove garlic, finely chopped
1 pound (500 g) small zucchini (courgettes), thinly sliced
1/4 cup (60 g) butter
1/2 cup (75 g) finely ground almonds
1 cup (250 ml) heavy (double) cream, heated
4 large eggs, separated
1/2 cup (60 g) freshly grated Cheddar or Gruyère cheese
Freshly ground black pepper

 CARBS 3g

Serves 6 • Preparation 15 minutes • Cooking 25–30 minutes
Difficulty 2

1. Preheat the oven to 350°F (180°C/gas 4). Grease 6 ramekins. Heat the oil in a large saucepan over low heat. Add the garlic and zucchini. Simmer without browning, stirring frequently, until completely soft, 10–15 minutes. Mash with a fork or potato masher and set aside.

2. Melt the butter in a small pan. Stir in the almonds. Add the cream and stir to make a thick sauce. Let bubble for 2 minutes then add to the zucchini, along with the egg yolks, cheese, and pepper. Beat well to get a nice sticky mixture.

3. Beat the egg whites in a large bowl until stiff. Fold into the zucchini mixture.

4. Divide evenly among the ramekins. Bake for 12–15 minutes, until risen and golden brown. Serve hot.

CHEESE & BROCCOLI soufflés

1   head broccoli, cut into florets
6   large eggs, separated
6   tablespoons freshly grated
      cheddar cheese + extra, for
      topping
      Salt and freshly ground black
      pepper

CARBS 1g Serves 4 • Preparation 15 minutes • Cooking 10–15 minutes
Difficulty 2

1. Preheat the oven to 400°F (200°C/gas 6). Grease four
   ramekins. Blanch the broccoli in boiling water for 2–3
   minutes, then drain well.

2. Put the broccoli in a blender and blend until finely
   chopped. Add the egg yolks and blend until combined.
   Pour into a bowl.

3. Beat the egg whites in a separate bowl until stiff peaks
   form. Fold the egg whites into the blended broccoli. Fold in
   the cheese. Season with salt and pepper.

4. Spoon the soufflé mixture into the prepared ramekins.
   Sprinkle with a little extra grated cheese.

5. Place the ramekins a baking sheet and bake for 8–10
   minutes, until risen and golden brown. Serve hot.

soups & salads

BEEF & VEGGIE soup

2 tablespoons extra-virgin olive oil

3 pounds (1.5 kg) stew beef, cut into small cubes

1 small onion, finely chopped

1 clove garlic, finely chopped

6 cups (1.5 liters) water

4 tomatoes, peeled and chopped

2 tablespoons finely chopped parsley + extra leaves, to garnish

$^1/_2$ teaspoon chili powder

1 bay leaf

4 stalks celery, coarsely chopped

1 very small cabbage (about 12 ounces/350 g), coarsely chopped

Salt and freshly ground black pepper

CARBS 4g • Serves 8 • Preparation 20 minutes • Cooking 2 hours • Difficulty 1

1. Heat the oil in a large soup pot over medium-high heat. Add the beef, onion, and garlic and sauté until the meat is browned all over, 5–8 minutes.

2. Add the water, tomatoes, parsley, chili, bay leaf, celery, and cabbage. Season with salt and pepper. Cover the pan and simmer over low heat until the meat is very tender, about 2 hours.

3. Ladle into bowls or cups, garnish with the extra parsley, and serve hot.

If you liked this recipe, you will love these as well.

TEX-MEX chili soup

DEVILISH beef soup

BEEF stew

CRESS & FENNEL miso

2 tablespoons vegetable oil

1 pound (500 g) fennel bulbs, cut into wedges and finely sliced

1 carrot, cut into very thin strips

Whites of 2 leeks, trimmed and thinly sliced

1 (1-inch/2.5-cm) piece ginger, peeled and finely chopped

1 clove garlic, finely chopped

1 small fresh red chili, seeded and finely chopped

1 teaspoon fennel seeds

Salt

3 tablespoons barley miso

6 cups (1.5 liters) boiling water

2 cup (100 g) watercress, stems removed + extra, to garnish

10 snow peas (mangetout), broken in half (optional)

1 tablespoon freshly squeezed lemon juice

CARBS 7g Serves 6 • Preparation 20 minutes • Cooking 30–35 minutes Difficulty 1

1. Heat the oil in a soup pot over medium heat. Add the fennel, carrot, and leeks and sauté until the vegetables are softened, 8–10 minutes. Stir in the ginger, garlic, chili, and fennel seeds. Season with salt and sauté over low heat for 10 minutes more.

2. Dissolve the miso in $1/2$ cup (120 ml) of boiling water. Stir the miso mixture and remaining water into the soup. Simmer until the vegetables are tender, 10–15 minutes. Add the watercress, snow peas, and lemon juice. Simmer for 3 minutes more.

3. Ladle into six soup bowls, garnish with the extra watercress leaves, and serve hot.

SHRIMP & TOFU SOUP with coconut milk

2 tablespoons vegetable oil

¼ cup (60 ml) laksa paste

4 cups (1 liter) fish stock

3 teaspoons grated palm sugar or brown sugar

2 cups (500 ml) coconut milk

20 green giant shrimp (king prawns), peeled and deveined, tails on

6 fried tofu puffs, quartered

2 cups (100 g) bean sprouts, trimmed

1 cucumber, halved lengthways and cut into thin strips

½ cup fresh mint leaves

½ cup fresh cilantro (coriander) leaves

1 lime, cut into wedges

CARBS 14g Serves 4 • Preparation 15 minutes • Cooking 8–10 minutes
Difficulty 1

1. Heat the oil in a wok over high heat until hot. Add the laksa paste and stir-fry until aromatic, about 1 minute Add the fish stock and palm sugar and bring to a boil. Stir in coconut milk and heat, stirring constantly, until hot.

2. Add the shrimp and tofu puffs. Simmer until the shrimp are pink, 3–4 minutes.

3. Ladle the soup into four bowls, dividing the shrimp and tofu evenly. Top with the bean sprouts, cucumber, mint, and cilantro. Serve hot with lime wedges.

Tex-Mex derives from the words Texas and Mexican and is used to describe the cooking style typical of Texas and other southern US states that lie close to the border with Mexico. Tex-Mex cuisine is often powerfully hot and spicy!

36

TEX-MEX chili soup

 CARBS 2g • Serves 6 • Preparation 15 minutes • Cooking 1½ hours • Difficulty 1

Soup

2 tablespoons extra-virgin olive oil
2 pounds (1 kg) ground (minced) lean beef
1 small onion, finely chopped
2 cloves garlic, finely chopped
2–3 teaspoons hot chili powder
1 teaspoon chipotle chili powder
3 teaspoons ground cumin
1 teaspoon cayenne pepper
1 teaspoon paprika
2 teaspoons salt
4 tomatoes, peeled and coarsely chopped
4 cups (1 liter) water

To Serve

2 tablespoons coarsely chopped cilantro (coriander)
½ small red onion, finely chopped
2 cherry tomatoes, thinly sliced
Freshly squeezed lemon juice

Soup

1. Heat the oil in a large soup pot over medium-high heat. Add the beef, onion, and garlic and sauté until browned, 5–8 minutes.

2. Add both chili powders, the cumin, cayenne, paprika, salt, tomatoes, and water and bring to a boil. Decrease the heat to low, partially cover the pan, and simmer for 1½ hours.

To Serve

1. Ladle into six serving bowls. Garnish each bowl with some cilantro, onion, cherry tomatoes, and lemon juice. Serve hot.

If you liked this recipe, you will love these as well.

BEEF & VEGGIE soup

DEVILISH beef soup

BEEF stew

PUMPKIN & PANCETTA soup

CARBS **2g** Serves 4 • Preparation 15 minutes • Cooking 25 minutes • Difficulty 1

8	ounces (250 g) sliced pancetta, coarsely chopped	1	pound (500 g) pumpkin (winter squash), peeled, seeded, and coarsely chopped
1	small onion, finely chopped		
3	cloves garlic, coarsely chopped	6	cups (1.5 liters) chicken stock

1. Place the pancetta in a large saucepan over medium heat and fry until crisp. Remove the pancetta and drain on paper towels.

2. Add the onion and garlic to the remaining oil in the saucepan and sauté until softened, 3–4 minutes.

3. Add the pumpkin and chicken stock and bring to a boil. Simmer for 12 minutes, or until the squash is tender.

4. Purée with a hand-held blender. Return to the heat, add the pancetta, and reheat for 2–3 minutes. Ladle into bowls and serve hot.

THAI chicken soup

CARBS **11g** Serves 4 • Preparation 20 minutes • Cooking 30 minutes • Difficulty 1

6	cups (1.5 liters) chicken stock		Freshly squeezed juice of 2 limes
3	tomatoes, chopped	2	tablespoons brown sugar
2	stalks lemongrass		
3	coriander roots, bruised	4	ounces (120 g) canned straw mushrooms
1	(1½-inch/4-cm) piece ginger, sliced	2	boneless skinless chicken breasts, sliced
2	red chilis, seeded and thinly sliced	12	shrimp (prawns), shelled, tails on
2	tablespoons Thai fish sauce	1	tablespoon fresh cilantro (coriander)

1. Put the stock in a soup pot over medium-high heat and bring to a boil. Add the tomatoes, lemongrass, coriander roots, ginger, and chilis. Reduce the heat to low and simmer for 20 minutes. Add the fish sauce, lime juice, sugar, and mushrooms and simmer for 5 minutes.

2. Add the chicken and shrimp and simmer until cooked through, 4–5 minutes. Remove the coriander roots and lemongrass. Garnish with cilantro and serve hot.

CARROT & ORANGE soup

CARBS **15g** Serves 4 • Preparation 15 minutes • Cooking 20–25 minutes • Difficulty 1

2	unwaxed oranges	½	cup finely chopped fresh cilantro (coriander) + extra leaves, to garnish
1	pound (500 g) carrots, grated		
1	small onion, sliced		
4	cups (1 liter) vegetable stock		

1. Use a sharp knife to remove the zest from the oranges—outer orange part only. Slice thinly. Juice the oranges.

2. Combine the carrots, onion, orange juice, and zest in a large saucepan over medium heat. Add 2 cups (500 ml) of the stock and bring to a boil. Simmer for 10 minutes. Add the chopped cilantro to the soup.

3. Purée using a hand-held blender. Add the remaining 2 cups (500 ml) of stock to the soup and return to the heat. Simmer gently for 5 minutes. Garnish with the extra cilantro leaves and serve hot.

DEVILISH BEEF soup

CARBS **23g** Serves 4 • Preparation 20 minutes • Cooking 2 hours • Difficulty 1

3	tablespoons extra-virgin olive oil	2	stalks celery, sliced
1	small onion, sliced	1	carrot, finely chopped
3	cloves garlic, minced	2	red bell peppers (capsicums), sliced
2	red chilis, thinly sliced	5	tomatoes, diced
1	tablespoon sweet paprika	1	cup (200 g) canned corn (sweetcorn)
2	teaspoons cumin	8	cups (2 liters) water
1	teaspoon freshly ground black pepper	1	pound (500 g) beef cheek or brisket
1	teaspoon chili powder	2	tablespoons finely chopped fresh oregano
2	bay leaves		Salt

1. Heat the oil in a large soup pot over medium heat. Add the onion, garlic, and chilis and sauté until softened, 3–4 minutes. Add the paprika, cumin, pepper, chili powder, and bay leaves and sauté until fragrant, 1–2 minutes.

2. Add the celery, carrot, bell peppers, tomatoes, and corn and toss to coat. Pour in the water and bring to a boil. Add the beef and oregano and simmer over low heat until the beef is tender, about 2 hours.

3. Remove the beef from the pan. Shred with your fingertips, then return to the pan. Season with salt, return to a gentle simmer, and serve hot.

BROCCOLI SOUP with stilton

2   tablespoons extra-virgin olive oil
1   small onion, coarsely chopped
6   cups (1.5 liters) chicken stock
1   head broccoli, about 12 ounces (350 g), coarsely chopped
4   ounces (120 g) blue cheese, such as Stilton or Roquefort, crumbled
     Coarsely chopped fresh parsley, to garnish

CARBS 2g • Serves 4 • Preparation 15 minutes • Cooking 15 minutes • Difficulty 1

1. Heat the oil in a soup pot over medium heat. Add the onion and sauté until softened, 3–4 minutes. Add the vegetable stock and simmer for 2–3 minutes.

2. Add the broccoli and cook until just tender but still bright green, about 5 minutes. Remove from the heat and add half the cheese.

3. Purée the soup with a hand-held blender. Return to the heat and bring to a gentle simmer. Ladle into four serving bowls, garnish with the remaining cheese and the parsley, and serve hot.

COCK-A-LEEKIE soup

2 tablespoons butter
6 chicken drumsticks
6 leeks, chopped
4 slices bacon, rinds removed, chopped
8 cups (2 liters) chicken stock
1 bouquet garni, made with thyme, a bay leaf, and parsley
8 prunes
Salt and freshly ground black pepper
Fresh parsley, to garnish

 CARBS 10g

Serves 4 • Preparation 15 minutes • Cooking 1¼ hours • Difficulty 1

1. Melt the butter in a soup pot over medium heat. Add the chicken and sauté until they begin to brown. Add the bacon and leeks and sauté for 5 minutes.

2. Pour in the chicken stock and bring to a boil. Turn the heat down to low and simmer for a few minutes. Skim the surface with a small sieve to remove any scum that rises to the top. Add the bouquet garni and prunes, and season with salt and pepper. Simmer for 1 hour.

3. Remove and discard the bouquet garni and prunes. Remove the chicken drumsticks and separate the meat from the bones. Stir the meat back into the soup.

4. Ladle the soup into four serving bowls and garnish with parsley. Serve hot.

Serve this chicken salad as a light lunch. Delicious and nourishing, it will keep you going through the afternoon.

CHICKEN salad

4	boneless skinless chicken breast halves
2	tablespoons extra-virgin olive oil
	Salt and freshly ground black pepper
½	cup (120 ml) mayonnaise
½	cup (120 ml) sour cream
1	tablespoon finely chopped fresh dill + extra, to garnish
1	tablespoon finely chopped fresh basil + extra, to garnish
2	cloves garlic, minced
1	small red onion, finely chopped
1	red bell pepper (capsicum), seeded and thinly sliced
4	stalks celery, thinly sliced
1	cup (150 g) red seedless grapes, halved
½	cup (60 g) sliced almonds

 CARBS 10g

Serves 4 • Preparation 15 minutes • Cooking 8–10 minutes
Difficulty 1

1. Preheat a grill pan (griddle) over medium-high heat. Brush the chicken breasts with the oil and season with salt and pepper. Grill the chicken until tender and cooked through, 8–10 minutes. Let cool a little, then slice thinly.

2. Mix the mayonnaise and sour cream in a small bowl with the dill, basil, and garlic.

3. Combine the chicken in a large shallow bowl with the onion, bell pepper, celery, grapes, and almonds. Spoon the mayonnaise mixture over the top and toss a little to mix.

4. Garnish with the extra dill and basil and serve.

If you liked this recipe, you will love these as well.

CHICKEN waldorf

CHICKEN & CORN
salad

HOISEN DUCK
with cucumber

NIÇOISE salad

Salad

10	medium firm tomatoes, each cut into 8 wedges
	Salt
3	cups (150 g) mixed salad greens
1	red bell pepper (capsicum), seeded and cut into thin strips
8	ounces (250 g) canned tuna, drained
3	stalks celery, thinly sliced
3	shallots, finely chopped
12	black olives
6	salt-cured anchovy fillets
4	hard-boiled eggs, quartered

Vinaigrette

1/2	cup (120 ml) extra-virgin olive oil
2	tablespoons white wine vinegar
1	teaspoon Dijon mustard
	Salt and freshly ground black pepper

 CARBS 7g • Serves 4 • Preparation 15 minutes + 1 hour to drain • Difficulty 1

Salad

1. Place the tomatoes in a colander and sprinkle lightly with salt. Let stand for 1 hour to drain. Arrange the salad greens in four salad bowls with the tomatoes around the edges. Put the bell pepper, tuna, celery, and shallots in the center. Arrange the olives and anchovy fillets on top. Garnish with the wedges of boiled egg.

Vinaigrette

1. Whisk the oil, vinegar, mustard, salt, and pepper in a small bowl. Drizzle over the salad and serve.

WINTER salad

2   large ripe oranges
1   fennel bulb, very thinly sliced
8–12   large thin slices prosciutto
$^1/_4$ cup (60 ml) extra-virgin olive oil
       Salt and freshly ground black pepper

CARBS
9g

Serves 4 • Preparation 10 minutes • Difficulty 1

1. Peel the oranges. Use a very sharp knife to remove the bitter white pith from the oranges, working over a bowl to catch the juice. Reserve the juice for the dressing. Slice the oranges thinly crosswise, removing any seeds.

2. Divide the oranges evenly among four individual serving plates. Top with the fennel and prosciutto.

3. Drizzle with the oil and orange juice. Season with salt and pepper and serve.

This recipe will serve eight people as a starter or four people as a main course. If you like spicy food, drizzle with some extra chili sauce.

BEEF & LETTUCE cups

14 ounces (400 g) rump steak, cut into thin strips
2   tablespoons light soy sauce
1   tablespoon dry sherry
1   small piece fresh ginger, peeled and grated
1   clove garlic, finely chopped
2   pinches of five-spice powder
1   teaspoon Thai chili sauce
1   tablespoon sesame oil
6   scallions (green onions), sliced diagonally
1   small red bell pepper (capsicum), seeded and diced
8   crisp cup-shaped lettuce leaves, chilled, to serve
    Sprigs of cilantro (coriander), to garnish

 CARBS 5g Serves 4 • Preparation 10 minutes + 1 hour to marinate • Cooking 3–5 minutes. • Difficulty 1

1. Put the steak in a bowl. Add the soy sauce, sherry, ginger, garlic, five-spice powder, and chili sauce. Mix well, then cover and marinate in the refrigerator for 1 hour, stirring occasionally.

2. Heat the oil in a large wok. Add the scallions and bell pepper and stir-fry for 1 minute.

3. Add the beef mixture and stir-fry until the meat is cooked to your liking, 2–4 minutes.

4. Spoon into the chilled lettuce cups, garnish with cilantro, and serve hot.

If you liked this recipe, you will love these as well.

STEAK SALAD
with papaya

SOUVLAKI

GROUND BEEF
kebabs

CHEESE & GRAPEFRUIT salad

CARBS **4g** Serves 4 • Preparation 10 minutes • Difficulty 1

Salad
4	cups (200 g) baby spinach leaves
4	ounces (120 g) Parmesan cheese, in shavings
1	grapefruit, peeled and divided into segments

Dressing
1/2	cup (90 ml) extra-virgin olive oil
	Freshly squeezed juice of 1/2 lemon
1	tablespoon snipped fresh chives
	Salt and freshly ground black pepper

Salad

1. Divide the spinach evenly among four individual serving plates. Top with the cheese and grapefruit.

Dressing

1. Whisk the oil, lemon juice, and chives in a small bowl. Season with salt and pepper. Drizzle the dressing over the salads and serve.

CHICKEN waldorf

CARBS **5g** Serves 4 • Preparation 20 minutes + 1¼ hours to cool Cooking 10–15 minutes • Difficulty 1

4	boneless, skinless chicken breast halves Pinch of mixed herbs Salt	2	tablespoons freshly squeezed lemon juice
2	crisp red apples, cored and cut into bite-size cubes	2	stalks celery, sliced
		1/2	cup (60 g) walnuts, coarsely chopped
		1/2	cup (120 ml) full fat mayonnaise

1. To poach the chicken, pour 4 cups (1 liter) of water into a medium saucepan. Bring to a boil and add the chicken, mixed herbs, and salt. Simmer until the chicken is cooked, 10–15 minutes. Let sit in the cooking water for 15 minutes. Drain and set aside to cool completely, at least 1 hour. Cut the cooled chicken into bite-size cubes.

2. Drizzle the apples with the lemon juice to prevent them from turning brown.

3. Combine the chicken, apples, celery, and walnuts in a large salad bowl. Add the mayonnaise, toss gently, and serve.

ORANGE & ARTICHOKE salad

CARBS **15g** Serves 4 • Preparation 15 minutes • Difficulty 1

4	fresh artichokes Freshly squeezed juice of 1 lemon	1	tablespoon finely chopped fresh parsley
2	oranges, peeled and divided into segments	1/3	cup (90 ml) extra-virgin olive oil
5	ounces (150 g) aged pecorino cheese, flaked		Salt and freshly ground black pepper

1. Clean the artichokes by trimming the stalks and cutting off the top third of the leaves. Remove the tough outer leaves by pulling them down and snapping them off at the base. Cut the artichokes in half and use a sharp knife to remove any fuzzy core. Cut the artichokes into thin wedges.

2. Put the artichokes in a large salad bowl and drizzle with half the lemon juice. This will stop them from turning brown.

3. Place the oranges, pecorino, and parsley in a large salad bowl. Drain the artichokes and add to the bowl.

4. Drizzle with the oil and remaining lemon juice and season with salt and pepper. Toss gently and serve.

FENNEL & PARMESAN salad

CARBS **3g** Serves 4 • Preparation 10 minutes • Cooking 5 minutes • Difficulty 1

6	tablespoons pine nuts	1/4	cup (60 ml) extra-virgin olive oil
2	fennel bulbs, with tops	2	tablespoons freshly squeezed lemon juice
4	ounces (120 g) Parmesan cheese, flaked		Salt and freshly ground black pepper

1. Toast the pine nuts in a small frying pan over medium heat until pale golden brown, 3–4 minutes. Shake the pan often during cooking so that they don't burn. Set aside to cool a little.

2. Strip the tough outer leaves from the fennel bulbs. Slice the tender inner leaves thinly lengthwise. Place on four serving plates. Sprinkle with the fennel tops to garnish.

3. Top with the Parmesan and pine nuts. Season with the oil, lemon juice, salt, and pepper, toss gently, and serve.

CHICKEN & CORN salad

4 ears (cobs) fresh corn (sweetcorn), with husks

¼ cup (60 g) butter, softened

2 tablespoons harissa

Finely grated zest and juice of 1 untreated lemon

2 tablespoons finely chopped fresh parsley

Salt and freshly ground black pepper

2 boneless skinless chicken breasts

4 tablespoons (60 ml) extra-virgin olive oil

Pinch of cayenne pepper

1 red bell pepper (capsicum), seeded and sliced

1 avocado, pitted and sliced

2 cups (100 g) lamb's lettuce

Small bunch fresh chives, snipped

CARBS 18g

Serves 4 • Preparation 30 minutes • Cooking 20–30 minutes
Difficulty 2

1. Peel back the husks on the ears of corn, leaving the leaves attached at the base. Blend the butter, harissa, lemon zest, and parsley in a bowl. Season with salt and pepper. Smear over the corn, then re-cover with the leaves and tie each ear with kitchen string.

2. Preheat a grill pan (griddle) to hot. Grill the corn, turning often, until blackened and tender, 15–20 minutes. Set aside.

3. Brush the chicken with 1 tablespoon of oil, season with salt, pepper, and cayenne. Grill until cooked through, 3–5 minutes on each side. Set aside.

4. Combine the bell pepper, avocado, and lamb's lettuce in a bowl and toss. Whisk the remaining oil with the lemon juice, salt, and pepper in a bowl. Drizzle over the salad. Slice the chicken into strips and add to the salad.

5. Remove the string and husks from the corn and use a sharp knife to strip off the kernels. Add to the salad. Toss well, sprinkle with the chives, and serve warm.

STEAK SALAD with papaya

Salad

1¼ pounds (600 g) tenderloin (fillet steak), trimmed

1 tablespoon finely chopped fresh rosemary

Salt

¼ teaspoon cayenne pepper

2 tablespoons butter

1 small papaya, peeled, seeded, and cut into bite-size cubes

1 small red onion, thinly sliced

1 cup (50 g) mixed salad greens

Dressing

5 tablespoons (75 ml) extra-virgin olive oil

2 tablespoons red wine vinegar

Salt and freshly ground black pepper

 Serves 4 • Preparation 15 minutes • Cooking 2–5 minutes • Difficulty 1

CARBS 3g

Salad

1. Cut the steak into thin slices. Sprinkle with the rosemary, salt, and cayenne pepper.

2. Heat the butter in a large frying pan over high heat. Add the steak and sauté until cooked to your liking, 2–5 minutes.

Dressing

1. Whisk the oil, vinegar, salt, and pepper in a small bowl.

2. Mix the steak, papaya, onion, and greens in a bowl. Drizzle with the dressing and toss well. Divide the salad evenly among four serving dishes and serve.

seafood & meat

SEAFOOD salad

1 pound (500 g) clams,
in shell

1 pound (500 g) mussels,
in shell

1 pound (500 g) octopus,
cleaned

14 ounces (400 g) calamari,
cleaned and sliced into rings

1 pound (500 g) raw shrimp
(green prawns)

1/2 cup (120 ml) extra-virgin
olive oil

Freshly squeezed juice
of 1/2 lemon

2 cloves garlic, finely chopped

2 tablespoons finely chopped
fresh parsley

Salt and freshly ground black
pepper

1/2 teaspoon crushed dried chilis
or red pepper flakes
(optional)

 Serves 6 • Preparation 30 minutes + 2¼ hours to soak, cool & chill
Cooking 1 hour • Difficulty 2

1. Soak the clams and mussels in a large bowl of cold water
for at least 1 hour. Pull the beards off the mussels. Scrub
well and rinse in abundant cold water.

2. Place the octopus in a large pot of cold water and bring
to a boil over high heat. Lower the heat to a gentle simmer
and cook until tender, about 1 hour.

3. Add the calamari rings and shrimp to the pot with the
octopus just before it is ready. Simmer until the shrimp
are pink, 2–4 minutes. Let the seafood cool in the cooking
water for 15 minutes. Drain and set aside to cool.

4. Shell the shrimp and place in a salad bowl with the
calamari. Chop the octopus into bite-size pieces and add
to the salad bowl.

5. Put the clams and mussels in a large frying pan over
medium heat. Cover with a lid and cook until they are all
open. Discard any that do not open. Remove the mollusks
from their shells and add to the salad bowl.

6. Whisk the oil, lemon juice, garlic, parsley, salt, pepper, and
chilis, if using, in a bowl. Pour over the salad and toss well.

7. Chill in the refrigerator for 1 hour before serving.

Swordfish are found in all the oceans and you will find it fresh during the warmer months of the year and frozen in the winter. It is an ideal fish for kebabs or grilling because the flesh stays in one piece.

SWORDFISH KEBABS with lemon

1¼ pounds (600 g) swordfish steaks, cut into 1-inch (2.5-cm) cubes

¼ cup (60 ml) extra-virgin olive oil

2 tablespoons freshly squeezed lemon juice

2 tablespoons fresh oregano leaves

1 clove garlic, finely chopped

Salt and freshly ground black pepper

CARBS 1g • Serves 4 • Preparation 10 minutes + 1 hour to marinate • Cooking 4–5 minutes • Difficulty 1

1. Thread the swordfish onto 8–12 bamboo or metal skewers.

2. Combine the oil, lemon juice, oregano, and garlic in a small bowl. Season with salt and pepper. Brush the skewers with this marinade, cover, and refrigerate for 1 hour.

3. Preheat a grill pan (griddle) or barbecue on high heat.

4. Grill the kebabs, turning frequently, until marked with lines and cooked through, 4–5 minutes. Serve hot.

If you liked this recipe, you will love these as well.

SEAFOOD salad

CAJUN fish

GRILLED TUNA STEAKS
with avocado

GRILLED scallops

CARBS **4g** • Serves 4 • Preparation 15 minutes • Cooking 4–5 minutes • Difficulty 2

2	medium tomatoes, peeled and diced	16	scallops, on the half shell
1	teaspoon freshly squeezed lemon juice	1/2	cup (120 g) butter, melted
1	tablespoon extra-virgin olive oil		Pinch of saffron threads, crushed
	Salt and freshly ground black pepper	1	tablespoon finely chopped fresh parsley

1. Preheat a broiler (overhead grill) on medium-high heat. Place the tomatoes in a small bowl with the lemon juice and oil. Season with salt and pepper.

2. Remove and discard the white chain from the side of each scallop. Rinse under cold water to remove any grit or sand.

3. Combine the butter and saffron in a small bowl. Dot the scallops with the saffron butter and top with the tomato mixture and parsley.

4. Place the shells under the broiler and cook until the scallops are firm and white, for 4–5 minutes. Serve hot.

GRILLED oysters

CARBS **4g** • Serves 4 • Preparation 15 minutes • Cooking 4–5 minutes • Difficulty 1

1–2	cups (200–400 g) rock salt	3	tablespoons Worcestershire sauce
24	shucked oysters on the half shell	2	tablespoons ketchup (tomato sauce)
6	ounces (180 g) pancetta, finely diced	1	tablespoon freshly squeezed lemon juice
1	purple shallot, finely diced		Freshly ground black pepper
1	large red chili, seeded and finely chopped	1	scallion (spring onion), thinly sliced

1. Preheat a broiler (overhead grill) on high heat. Spread the rock salt on a baking sheet and arrange the oysters in their shells on top.

2. Combine the pancetta, shallot, and chili in a small bowl and sprinkle over the oysters.

3. Mix the Worcestershire sauce, ketchup, and lemon juice in a small bowl. Spoon over the oysters and finish with freshly ground black pepper.

4. Broil (grill) the oysters until the pancetta is crisp, 4–5 minutes. Serve warm, with the sliced scallion.

SEA BASS with salsa

CARBS **8g** • Serves 6 • Preparation 25 minutes + 30 minutes to chill • Cooking 35–40 minutes • Difficulty 1

Tomato Salsa

2	pounds (1 kg) tomatoes	3	tablespoons chopped fresh cilantro (coriander)
4–6	medium red chilis		Freshly squeezed juice of 2 limes
1	red bell pepper (capsicum), halved		
5	cloves garlic, sliced	**Fish**	
7	tablespoons (100 ml) extra-virgin olive oil	6	fillets sea bass or sea bream (about 7 ounces /200 g each), with skin
1/2	teaspoon coarse salt		Lime wedges to serve
1	red onion, chopped		

Tomato Salsa

1. Preheat the oven to 425°F (220°C/gas 7). Put the tomatoes, chilis, and bell peppers, skin-side up, in a roasting pan. Sprinkle with the garlic. Drizzle with 1 tablespoon of oil and sprinkle with salt. Roast for 20–25 minutes, until the skins are lightly charred.

2. Chop in a food processor until coarsely blended. Mix in the onion, cilantro, remaining oil, and the lime juice.

Fish

1. Place in a shallow bowl, cover with half the salsa. Chill for 30 minutes. Preheat a grill pan (griddle) to hot. Grill the fillets until cooked through, 3–4 minutes. Serve hot with the reserved salsa and lime wedges.

CAJUN fish

CARBS **4g** • Serves 4 • Preparation 15 minutes • Cooking 4 minutes • Difficulty 1

Salad

2	cups (100 g) baby spinach leaves	**Fish**	
12	cherry tomatoes, halved	3	tablespoons extra-virgin olive oil
1	small red onion, sliced	3	tablespoons Cajun spice mix
2	tablespoons extra-virgin olive oil	4	(8-ounce/250-g) firm white fish fillets, such as snapper, cod, halibut, or monkfish
2	tablespoons freshly squeezed lemon juice	1	lemon, cut into wedges
1/2	teaspoon Dijon mustard		

Salad

1. Combine the spinach, tomatoes and onion in a medium bowl and set aside. Whisk the oil, lemon juice, and mustard in a small bowl. Pour the dressing over the salad and toss to combine. Set aside.

Fish

1. Preheat a large frying pan over medium-high heat.

2. Brush the fish with the oil and coat in the spice mix. Cook until blackened and the flesh flakes easily, about 2 minutes on each side.

3. Serve hot with the salad and lemon wedges.

SPICY FISH with broccoli

Freshly squeezed juice
of 4 limes

2 tablespoons Thai fish sauce

1 teaspoon sugar

2 small red chilis, seeded and
thinly sliced

2 long green chilis, seeded and
finely chopped

2 stalks lemongrass, shredded

1 tablespoon finely grated fresh
ginger

¹/₄ cup (60 ml) peanut oil

4 firm white fish fillets, such as
cod, haddock, snapper,
halibut, or whiting, skinned
(about 5 ounces/150 g each)

1 teaspoon light soy sauce

1 teaspoon rice wine

14 ounces (400 g) broccoli,
broken into small florets,
thicker stems cut in half

CARBS
3g

Serves 4 • Preparation 20 minutes • Cooking 10 minutes
Difficulty 2

1. Combine the lime juice, fish sauce, sugar, chilis, lemongrass, and ginger in a small bowl and set aside.

2. Heat the oil in a large frying pan over medium heat until hot and sizzling. Pour in the spice mixture. Add the fish and cook until golden underneath, 2–3 minutes. Turn the fish fillets and cook until the other side is golden, 1–2 minutes.

3. Transfer the fish to serving plates, drizzle with the soy sauce and rice wine, and set aside in a warm oven.

4. Increase the heat under the pan to medium-high. Add the broccoli and 1 tablespoon of water. Stir-fry for 3–4 minutes. Serve the fish hot with the broccoli.

GRILLED TUNA STEAKS with avocado

2   carrots, sliced

4   tuna steaks, about 7 ounces (200 g) each

5   tablespoons (75 ml) extra-virgin olive oil

     Salt and freshly ground black pepper

1   avocado, pitted and sliced

2   tablespoons freshly squeezed lemon juice

1   red chili, seeded and sliced

2   tablespoons coarsely chopped fresh cilantro (coriander)

 CARBS 3g

Serves 4 • Preparation 15 minutes • Cooking 8–10 minutes
Difficulty 1

1. Cook the carrots in lightly salted boiling water until just tender, 3–4 minutes. Drain and set aside.

2. Preheat a grill pan (griddle) over medium-high heat. Brush the tuna with 2 tablespoons of the oil and season with salt and pepper. Grill until just tender, about 2 minutes each side. Do not overcook or it will become dry.

3. Divide the carrots and avocado evenly among four serving plates. Top each one with a tuna steak.

4. Mix the remaining 3 tablespoons of oil with the lemon juice, chili, and cilantro. Drizzle a little over each dish, and serve.

Hoisen, or Hoisin, sauce, is a popular Chinese sauce used to flavor many dishes. Despite its name, which translates as "seafood," it does not contain fish. It is traditionally made with sweet potato, sugar, vinegar, salt, and chilis. Hoisen sauce has quite a high carb count, so use sparingly if following a strict low-carb diet.

60

HOISEN DUCK with cucumber

Duck
4   duck breasts, with skin
2   tablespoons sea salt
2   teaspoons Chinese five-spice powder

Cucumber Salad
1   continental cucumber
2   celery sticks
4   scallions (spring onions), thinly sliced
2   cups (50 g) curly endive lettuce
3/4 cup cilantro (coriander) leaves
1/2 cup bean sprouts
2   tablespoons freshly squeezed lime juice
1   tablespoon extra-virgin olive oil
1   teaspoon sesame oil

Hoisen Sauce
3   tablespoons hoisen sauce
2   tablespoons soy sauce
2   teaspoons sesame oil
1   clove garlic, minced
1   teaspoon finely grated ginger

 CARBS 4g Serves 6 • Preparation 30 minutes + 1 hour to chill • Cooking 12–15 minutes • Difficulty 2

Duck

1. Score the skin of the duck breasts at $1/4$ inch (5 mm) intervals to form a criss-cross pattern. Rub the salt over the skin. Transfer to a plate, skin-side up, and chill for 1 hour.

Cucumber Salad

1. Cut the cucumber in half lengthwise and scrape out the seeds. Cut into thirds crosswise and thinly slice into strips. Cut the celery and scallions to a similar size. Place the cucumber, celery, scallions, lettuce, cilantro, and bean sprouts in a bowl. Whisk the lime juice, olive oil, and sesame oil in a small bowl. Pour over the salad and toss to coat.

2. Preheat a grill pan (griddle) or a flat-grill on a barbecue on medium-low heat.

3. Rinse the salt off the duck and pat dry with paper towels. Sprinkle the Chinese five spice mix over the duck and grill, skin-side down first, until crisp and golden brown, about 8 minutes. Turn the breasts over and grill until cooked to your liking, 4–5 minutes. Transfer to a plate, cover, and set aside in a warm place to rest for 5 minutes.

Hoisen Sauce

1. Combine the hoisen sauce, soy sauce, sesame oil, garlic, and ginger in a medium bowl.

2. Thickly slice the duck and serve hot with hoisen sauce and cucumber salad.

CHICKEN WINGS with blue cheese

Wings

1	large egg
1	cup (250 ml) cider vinegar
$^1/_2$	cup (120 ml) extra-virgin olive oil
1	teaspoon salt
$^1/_2$	teaspoon freshly ground black pepper
2	cloves garlic, finely chopped
2	pounds (1 kg) chicken wings, separated at joint, and wing tips discarded

Blue Cheese Dipping Sauce

1	cup (250 ml) mayonnaise
$^1/_2$	cup (120 ml) sour cream
7	ounces (200 g) blue cheese, crumbled
1	scallion (green onion), chopped
1	tablespoon freshly squeezed lemon juice
2	cloves garlic, finely chopped

CARBS 2g Serves 6 • Preparation 20 minutes • Cooking 30 minutes
Difficulty 1

Wings

1. Preheat the oven to 400F (200°C/gas 6). Beat the egg in a medium bowl. Add the vinegar, oil, salt, pepper, and garlic. Stir until well combined.

2. Dip the chicken in the marinade and arrange in a large baking pan. Bake for 30 minutes, turning and brushing with marinade several times, until crisp and golden.

Blue Cheese Dipping Sauce

1. Mix the mayonnaise, sour cream, blue cheese, scallion, lemon juice and garlic in a small bowl.

2. Serve the wings hot with the dipping sauce.

CHICKEN WINGS with sesame

Marinade

1/4	cup (60 ml) honey
1/4	cup (60 ml) soy sauce
1	tablespoon sesame oil
2	teaspoons finely grated ginger
2	cloves garlic, finely chopped

Chicken

16	chicken wings
1	tablespoon sesame seeds
1/2	cup fresh cilantro (coriander), to garnish

CARBS 13g • Serves 6 • Preparation 15 minutes + 4–12 hours to marinate
Cooking 8–12 minutes • Difficulty 1

Marinade

1. Combine the honey, soy sauce, sesame oil, ginger, and garlic in a small saucepan. Warm over low heat, stirring to combine, until the honey has melted. Transfer to a medium bowl and set aside to cool. Add the chicken wings and toss to coat. Sprinkle with sesame seeds. Cover and refrigerate for at least 4 hours or overnight.

Chicken

1. Preheat a grill pan (griddle) or barbecue over high heat. Oil a grill rack. Place the chicken wings on the prepared rack.

2. Grill the chicken wings until tender and cooked through, 4–6 minutes on each side. Serve hot, garnished with the cilantro.

Cajun cuisine is named after the French-speaking migrants who were deported from Canada and settled in Louisiana, in the United States. Their distinctive cooking style, characterized by the use of aromatic vegetables such as bell peppers, onion, and celery, is still very much alive today.

HOT & SPICY cajun chicken

Cajun Spice Mix

1/4	cup (60 ml) vegetable oil
3	tablespoons freshly squeezed lemon juice
1	tablespoon garlic powder
1	tablespoon onion powder
2	teaspoons hot paprika
2	teaspoons cayenne pepper
1	teaspoon dried thyme
1	teaspoon dried oregano
1	teaspoon ground cumin
1	teaspoon white pepper
1	teaspoon freshly ground black pepper
8	chicken thighs, bone in, slashed

Salad

2	avocadoes, sliced lengthwise
1	small fennel bulb, trimmed and thinly sliced
2	cups (100 g) watercress
1	ruby red grapefruit, peeled and segmented
1	lime, peeled and segmented
1	tablespoon freshly squeezed lime juice
1	teaspoon Dijon mustard
2	tablespoons extra-virgin olive oil
	Salt and freshly cracked black pepper

CARBS 8g · Serves 4 · Preparation 15 minutes + 4–12 hours to marinate Cooking 15–20 minutes · Difficulty 1

Cajun Spice Mix

1. Combine the oil, lemon juice, garlic powder, onion powder, paprika, cayenne, thyme, oregano, cumin, white pepper, and black pepper in a medium bowl. Add the chicken and toss to coat, rubbing the spice mix into the slashes and under the skin. Cover and refrigerate for 4 hours or overnight.

2. Preheat a grill over high heat. Oil a grill rack. Place the chicken thighs on the prepared rack.

Salad

1. Put the avocado, fennel, watercress, grapefruit, and lime in a bowl. Combine the lime juice and mustard in a small bowl. Gradually whisk in the oil and season with salt and pepper.

2. Grill the chicken, skin-side down first, until golden brown and cooked through, 7–8 minutes on each side. Serve hot with the salad.

If you liked this recipe, you will love these as well.

CHICKEN WINGS
with sesame

JAMAICAN JERK
drumsticks

SPICY CHICKEN cakes

CHICKEN yakitori

Sauce

¹⁄₄	cup (60 ml) shoyu (Japanese soy sauce)
3	tablespoons sake
2	tablespoons mirin
1¹⁄₂	tablespoons sugar

Chicken

1	pound (500 g) chicken thigh fillets, skin off, cut into ³⁄₄-inch (2-cm) cubes
2	tablespoons vegetable oil

 CARBS 10g • Serves 4 • Preparation 15 minutes + 1 hour to chill • Cooking 8–12 minutes • Difficulty 1

Sauce

1. Combine the shoyu, sake, mirin, and sugar in a small saucepan and bring to a boil. Decrease the heat and simmer until the sugar has dissolved and the sauce has thickened slightly, about 2 minutes. Transfer to a small bowl and set aside to cool.

Chicken

1. Thread the chicken onto small metal or bamboo skewers. Brush with half the sauce, cover, and refrigerate for 1 hour.

2. Preheat a grill pan (griddle) or a barbecue on medium heat.

3. Drizzle the oil on the grill. Cook the skewers, basting occasionally with the remaining sauce, until cooked through, 8–12 minutes. Serve hot.

JAMAICAN JERK drumsticks

Jerk Seasoning

3	purple shallots, coarsely chopped
2	scallions (spring onions) coarsely chopped
1-2	scotch bonnet or habanero chilis, seeded and coarsely chopped
2	cloves garlic, coarsely chopped
2	tablespoons light brown sugar
1	tablespoon ground pimento berries
2	teaspoons dried thyme leaves
1	teaspoon ground cinnamon
$^{1}/_{2}$	teaspoon ground nutmeg
$^{1}/_{4}$	teaspoon ground cloves
2	tablespoons white wine vinegar

Chicken

8	chicken drumsticks, slashed
1	tablespoon vegetable oil

 CARBS 7g • Serves 4 • Preparation 15 minutes + 1 hour to chill • Cooking 10–15 minutes • Difficulty 1

Jerk Seasoning

1. Put the shallots, scallions, chilis, garlic, brown sugar, pimento, thyme, cinnamon, nutmeg, and cloves in a small food processor and blend to form a coarse paste. Add the vinegar and oil and blend until smooth.

Chicken

1. Coat the drumsticks in the jerk seasoning and oil, rubbing them into the slashes and under the skin. Cover and refrigerate for 1 hour.

2. Preheat a grill pan (griddle) or a barbecue on medium heat. Grill the chicken drumsticks, turning frequently, until lightly charred and cooked through, 10–15 minutes. Serve hot.

BAKED CHICKEN & fennel

 Serves 4 • Preparation 10 minutes • Cooking 35 minutes • Difficulty 1

4	chicken leg quarters	1/2	cup (50 g) black olives, pitted (stoned)
3	tablespoons extra-virgin olive oil	1	tablespoon coarsely chopped fresh rosemary
6	baby fennel, cut in half lengthwise		

1. Preheat the oven to 350°F (180°C/gas 4).

2. Fry the chicken in 2 tablespoons of oil in a large frying pan over medium-high heat for 5 minutes, until browned all over.

3. Transfer the chicken to a baking dish. Arrange the fennel and olives in the baking dish with the chicken. Sprinkle with the rosemary and drizzle with the remaining 1 tablespoon of oil.

4. Bake for about 30 minutes, until cooked through. Serve hot.

SPICY CHICKEN cakes

 Serves 4 • Preparation 15 minutes + 1 hour to chill Cooking 8–10 minutes • Difficulty 1

1 1/4	pounds (600 g) ground (minced) chicken	2	tablespoons fresh cilantro (coriander)
1/4	cup (30 g) finely ground almonds	2	scallions (spring onions), chopped
1	large egg	2	red birds' eye chilis
2	cloves garlic	2	tablespoons vegetable oil
2	teaspoons ginger	1	cup (250 ml) sweet chili sauce
1/2	teaspoon salt		Lime wedges, to serve
1/4	teaspoon black pepper		

1. Chop the chicken, almonds, egg, garlic, ginger, salt, and pepper in a food processor. Transfer to a bowl, add the cilantro, scallions, and chilis and mix to combine. Shape into 12 even-size cakes. Place on a large plate, cover, and refrigerate for 1 hour.

2. Preheat a grill pan (griddle) or a barbecue on medium heat. Drizzle the oil on the grill plate and grill the chicken cakes, 4–5 minutes on each side.

3. Serve hot with the sweet chili sauce and lime.

CHICKEN with pancetta

 Serves 4 • Preparation 15 minutes + 1 hour to marinate • Cooking 20 minutes • Difficulty 1

4	boneless, skinless chicken breasts	2	cups (500 ml) heavy (double) cream
1/3	cup (90 ml) sun-dried tomato pesto	6	cups (300 g) baby spinach leaves
12	slices pancetta		

1. Coat the chicken with the pesto in a large bowl. Cover with plastic wrap (cling film) and refrigerate for 1 hour.

2. Dry-fry the pancetta in a medium saucepan over medium heat for 3 minutes until crispy. Remove and set aside.

3. Pour in the cream and bring to a boil. Decrease the heat and simmer over low heat until the cream has reduced by half.

4. Meanwhile, place a grill pan over medium-high heat. Grill the chicken for 5 minutes on each side until cooked through. Let rest in a warm place for 5 minutes.

5. Add the spinach to the cream and cook until wilted. Stir in the pancetta. Serve the chicken hot with the creamy spinach.

STUFFED CHICKEN breasts

 Serves 4 • Preparation 15 minutes • Cooking 10–12 minutes • Difficulty 2

4	ounces (120 g) feta cheese, crumbled	3	cups (150 g) arugula (rocket) leaves
1/4	cup (60 ml) olive tapenade	1/4	cup (60 ml) balsamic vinegar
4	boneless, skinless chicken breasts		

1. Mix the feta and tapenade in a small bowl.

2. Make a single cut in the chicken breasts to create a pocket and stuff with the feta mixture. Secure with toothpicks.

3. Place a large nonstick frying pan over medium heat. Cook the chicken, 10–12 minutes, until golden brown on the outside and cooked through.

4. Place the arugula in a medium bowl and drizzle with the balsamic vinegar. Slice the chicken and serve hot with the arugula.

SURF & TURF with tarragon butter

Tarragon Butter

2	teaspoons extra-virgin olive oil
2	purple shallots, finely chopped
1	cup (250 g) salted butter
2	tablespoons finely chopped fresh tarragon leaves

Steaks

4	(6-ounce/180-g) beef tenderloin (fillet) steaks
12	shrimp (prawns), peeled, heads removed, tails left on
3	tablespoons extra-virgin olive oil
	Salt and freshly ground black pepper

CARBS 1g • Serves 4 • Preparation 15 minutes + 1 hour to chill • Cooking 10 minutes • Difficulty 1

Tarragon Butter

1. Heat the oil in a small frying pan over low heat. Add the shallots and sauté until softened, 3–4 minutes. Transfer to a small bowl and set aside to cool.

2. Beat the shallots, butter, and tarragon in a bowl until combined. Lay a 12-inch (30-cm) long piece of parchment paper on a work surface. Spoon the butter onto the paper and roll up into an 8-inch (20-cm) long log. Chill for 1 hour.

Steaks

1. Preheat a grill pan (griddle) or barbecue on high heat. Brush the steaks and shrimp with the oil. Season with salt and pepper. Grill the steaks for 3–4 minutes on each side. Transfer to a plate, cover, and set aside in a warm place for 5 minutes.

2. Grill the shrimp until colored, about 1 minute on each side.

3. To serve, cut slices of tarragon butter and place one on top of each steak. Stack with the shrimp and serve hot.

KOREAN-STYLE short ribs

2 tablespoons white wine vinegar

½ cup (120 ml) ketchup

¼ cup (60 ml) soy sauce

2 tablespoons honey

2 teaspoons finely grated ginger

2 cloves garlic, finely chopped

3 pounds (1.5 kg) beef short ribs, cut crosswise

 CARBS 7g • Serves 8 • Preparation 15 minutes + 4–12 hours to marinate
Cooking 15–20 minutes • Difficulty 1

1. Combine all ingredients, except for the meat, in a large bowl. Add the beef ribs and toss to coat. Cover and refrigerate for at least 4 hours, or overnight.

2. Preheat a barbecue or indoor grill over high heat. Oil a grill rack.

3. Remove the ribs from the marinade, reserving the marinade. Place them on the prepared rack.

4. Grill the ribs, basting occasionally with the marinade, until charred and cooked through, 6–10 minutes on each side for medium-rare. Serve hot.

Souvlaki is a traditional Greek dish and has been around since ancient times. It is mentioned in the works of Aristotle and Aristophanes, among others. Served with salad and full-fat yogurt, it is the perfect dish for a low-carb diet.

SOUVLAKI

Skewers

3	pounds (1.5 kg) lamb leg or shoulder, trimmed of fat, cut into chunks
1/3	cup (90 ml) extra-virgin olive oil
1/3	cup (90 ml) dry red wine
2	tablespoons finely chopped fresh oregano
	Finely grated zest and juice of 2 unwaxed lemons
3	cloves garlic, finely chopped
	Salt and freshly ground black pepper

To Serve

2	cups (100 g) baby salad greens
20	cherry tomatoes, halved
1	cucumber, cut into chunks
2	tablespoons coarsely chopped fresh mint
	Freshly squeezed lemon juice
	Salt and freshly ground black pepper
1	cup (250 ml) plain, Greek-style yogurt

 CARBS 4g Serves 8 • Preparation 15 minutes + 12 hours to marinate • Cooking 10–15 minutes • Difficulty 1

Skewers

1. Put the lamb in a large bowl. Add the oil, wine, oregano, lemon zest and juice, garlic, salt, and pepper. Mix until all the lamb is coated. Cover and marinate in the refrigerator overnight.

2. Remove the lamb from the marinade and thread onto eight metal or wooden skewers.

3. Preheat a barbecue or indoor grill. Grill until the lamb is cooked to your liking, 10–15 minutes.

To Serve

1. Toss the salad greens, cherry tomatoes, cucumber, mint, and lemon juice together. Season with salt and pepper and toss again. Cover each serving plate with some salad, top with a skewer, and finish with a dollop or two of yogurt.

If you liked this recipe, you will love these as well.

GROUND BEEF
kebabs

INDONESIAN
beef satay

GREEK LAMB
klefto

GROUND BEEF kebabs

1½ pounds (750 g) ground
    (minced) beef
½   cup (75 g) finely ground
    almonds
1   large egg, lightly beaten
4   ounces (120 g) feta cheese,
    crumbled
2   cloves garlic, finely chopped
1   small red onion, finely grated
2   teaspoons ground cumin
    Finely grated zest of 1
    unwaxed lemon
2   tablespoons finely chopped
    fresh parsley
2   tablespoons finely chopped
    fresh oregano
4   tomatoes, cut into wedges
    Mixed salad greens, to serve

 CARBS 4g Serves 6 • Preparation 15 minutes • Cooking 6–8 minutes • Difficulty 1

1. Mix the beef, almonds, egg, feta, garlic, onion, cumin, lemon zest, parsley, and oregano in a large bowl. Shape the mixture into eight long sausages. Thread the sausages onto metal skewers.

2. Place a grill pan (griddle) over medium-high heat. Grill the kebabs until cooked to your liking, turning from time to time, 6–8 minutes.

3. Serve the kebabs hot with the tomatoes and salad.

BEEF stew

1½ pounds (750 g) stew beef, cut into bite-size cubes
2 teaspoons salt
1 teaspoon freshly ground black pepper
1 teaspoon paprika
1 tablespoon finely chopped fresh thyme
2 tablespoons extra-virgin olive oil
2 tablespoons butter
1 small onion, finely chopped
2 cloves garlic, finely chopped
2 cups (500 ml) dry red wine
1 cup (250 ml) water
2 carrots, cut in small cubes
½ cup (75 g) frozen peas
2 tablespoons finely chopped fresh parsley

 CARBS 4g • Serves 6 • Preparation 15 minutes • Cooking 2 hours • Difficulty 1

1. Preheat the oven to 325°F (170°F/gas 3). Put the meat on a plate and season with the salt, pepper, paprika, and thyme. Toss well to coat.

2. Heat 1 tablespoon of oil in a Dutch oven over medium-high heat. Brown half the beef; transfer to a bowl. Repeat with remaining oil and beef. Set aside.

3. Melt the butter in the Dutch oven. Add the onion and garlic and sauté until softened, 3–4 minutes. Add the meat, wine, and water. Bring to a boil. Cover the Dutch oven and place in the oven. Cook for about 2 hours, until the beef is very tender. Add the carrots and peas after the meat has been in the oven for just over 1 hour.

4. Serve hot, sprinkled with the parsley.

These meatballs can also be served without the salad as an appetizer. In that case, these quantities will be enough for six to eight people.

76

BAKED MEATBALLS with salad

Meatballs

1	tablespoon extra-virgin olive oil
1	small onion, finely chopped
3	cloves garlic, finely chopped
8	ounces (250 g) ground (minced) veal
8	ounces (250 g) ground (minced) beef
8	ounces (250 g) ground (minced) pork
$\frac{1}{2}$	cup (60 g) freshly grated Parmesan cheese
2	large eggs
	Salt and freshly ground black pepper

To Serve

2	cups (100 g) mixed baby salad greens
6	cherry tomatoes, halved
1	small red onion, finely chopped
2	tablespoons coarsely chopped cilantro (coriander)
2	tablespoons extra-virgin olive oil
	Freshly squeezed lemon juice

CARBS 2g

Serves 8 • Preparation 15 minutes • Cooking 25–30 minutes
Difficulty 1

Meatballs

1. Preheat the oven to 375°F (190°C/gas 5).

2. Heat the oil in a large frying pan over medium heat. Add the onion and garlic and sauté until softened, 3–4 minutes.

3. Transfer to a bowl and mix in the ground meats, cheese, eggs, salt, and pepper. Roll into golf ball-size meatballs. Place on a baking pan..

4. Bake 20–25 minutes, until browned and cooked through.

To Serve

1. Toss the salad greens, cherry tomatoes, onion, cilantro, oil, and lemon juice in a medium bowl. Spread out on a serving platter. Top with the hot meatballs and serve hot.

If you liked this recipe, you will love these as well.

SPICY CHICKEN cakes

GROUND BEEF kebabs

CURRIED LAMB koftas

VEAL saltimbocca

4   tablespoons (60 g) butter
2   tablespoons extra-virgin olive oil
4   veal scallops (escalopes)
    Salt and freshly ground black pepper
1   cup (125 g) freshly grated fontina cheese
8   slices prosciutto (Parma ham)
12 leaves fresh sage + 1 tablespoon coarsely chopped
¼   cup (60 ml) beef stock
¼   cup (60 ml) dry white wine

CARBS 0g

Serves 6 • Preparation 15 minutes • Cooking 8–10 minutes
Difficulty 1

1. Melt 2 tablespoons of butter with the oil in a large frying pan over medium-high heat. Add the veal and fry until tender, about 2 minutes on each side. Season with salt and pepper.

2. Preheat the broiler (grill). Transfer the veal to a large roasting pan. Top each piece with the fontina, prosciutto, and sage leaves. Secure with toothpicks. Broil for about 2 minutes, until the cheese melts.

3. Melt the remaining butter in the frying pan in which you cooked the veal. Add the stock and wine. Bring to a boil. Simmer over low heat until the sauce reduces slightly, about 2 minutes. Stir in the chopped sage. Serve the veal hot with the pan juices.

STEAK with tomatoes & béarnaise sauce

Béarnaise Sauce

1/2	cup (120 ml) white vinegar
1	purple shallot, finely chopped
2	black peppercorns
4	large egg yolks
1	cup (250 g) butter, melted
2	tablespoons freshly squeezed lemon juice
1 1/2	tablespoons finely chopped fresh tarragon leaves
	Salt and freshly ground black pepper

Steak & Tomatoes

4	rib-eye steaks
3	tablespoons extra-virgin olive oil
	Salt and freshly ground black pepper
4	roma tomatoes, halved lengthwise
1	tablespoon dried oregano

CARBS 3g • Serves 4 • Preparation 15 minutes • Cooking 20 minutes Difficulty 2

Béarnaise Sauce

1. Put the vinegar, shallot, and peppercorns in a small saucepan and simmer until reduced to 2 tablespoons.

2. Whisk the vinegar reduction and egg yolks in a medium heatproof bowl. Rest the bowl over a saucepan of barely simmering water and whisk until thick. Remove from the heat and gradually add the butter in a thin and steady stream, whisking until thick. Stir in the lemon juice and tarragon, season with salt and pepper. Cover and set aside in a warm place.

Steak & Tomatoes

1. Preheat a barbecue or indoor grill on high heat. Brush the steaks with 2 tablespoons of oil. Season with salt and pepper. Drizzle the remaining 1 tablespoon of oil over the tomatoes and sprinkle with the oregano.

2. Grill the steaks until cooked to your liking, about 5 minutes on each side. Transfer to a plate, cover, and set aside in a warm place for 5 minutes.

3. Grill the tomatoes until slightly softened and golden brown, about 3 minutes each side. Serve the steaks hot with the tomatoes and Béarnaise sauce.

Satay, also known as sate, is a classic Indonesian dish made of marinated, grilled skewers served with a sauce. Any type of meat can be used, including chicken, mutton, pork, beef, or fish. Satay originally comes from the island of Java, where this peanut- and coconut-flavored sauce is popular.

INDONESIAN beef satay

Marinade

1 tablespoon coriander seeds
2 teaspoons cumin seeds
1 teaspoon black peppercorns
1 small onion, coarsely chopped
1 small chili, finely chopped
2 cloves garlic, minced
1 teaspoon finely grated ginger
1 teaspoon ground turmeric
1 teaspoon salt
1 teaspoon brown sugar
2 tablespoons peanut oil
2 tablespoons soy sauce
2 tablespoons freshly squeezed lime juice
1¼ pounds (600 g) beef rump, cut in small cubes
Fresh cilantro (coriander)

Satay Sauce

1 tablespoon peanut oil
2 purple shallots, finely chopped
4 cloves garlic, minced
2 small chilis, finely chopped
1 tablespoon finely grated ginger
1 teaspoon sweet paprika
1 cup (250 g) peanut butter
1 (14-ounce/400-ml) can coconut milk
3 tablespoons grated jaggery (palm sugar) or brown sugar
¼ cup (60 ml) freshly squeezed lime juice
2 tablespoons Thai fish sauce
1 tablespoon soy sauce

 CARBS 18g Serves 6 • Preparation 15 minutes + 1 hour to marinate • Cooking 20–25 minutes • Difficulty 1

Marinade

1. Dry-fry the coriander, cumin, and peppercorns in a small frying pan over medium-low heat until fragrant, about 1 minute. Transfer to a mortar and pestle or spice grinder and blend to make a fine powder.

2. Combine the spice powder, onion, chili, garlic, ginger, turmeric, salt, and sugar in a mortar and pestle or food processor and blend to make a coarse paste. Gradually add the peanut oil, soy sauce, and lime juice, blending until smooth.

3. Thread the beef onto metal or bamboo skewers. Brush with the marinade, cover, and refrigerate for 1 hour.

Satay Sauce

1. Heat the oil in a saucepan over medium heat. Add the shallots, garlic, chilis, and ginger and sauté until softened, 3–4 minutes. Stir in the paprika, peanut butter, coconut milk, and jaggery and bring to a boil. Decrease the heat to low, pour in the lime juice, fish sauce, and soy sauce and simmer until thickened, about 10 minutes. Keep warm.

2. Preheat a barbecue or indoor grill. Oil a grill rack. Place the skewers on the prepared rack. Grill the skewers until cooked to your liking, 3–5 minutes on each side.

3. Serve hot with the satay sauce and cilantro.

GREEK LAMB *klefto*

8   lamb chops, cut about ¹/₂ inch (1.5 cm) thick

12 shallots, unpeeled

2   cups (500 ml) dry white wine

Finely shredded zest and juice of 2 unwaxed lemons

3   tablespoons fresh oregano leaves

 CARBS 4g Serves 4 • Preparation 10 minutes • Cooking 2 hours • Difficulty 1

1. Preheat the oven to 300°F (150°C/gas 2). Put all the ingredients in a large baking dish. Cover with aluminum foil. Bake for about 2 hours, until the lamb is tender.

2. Remove from the oven. Pour the cooking juices into a small saucepan. Bring to a boil over high heat and cook until reduced by half. Arrange the lamb and shallots in serving bowls. Drizzle with the cooking juices and serve hot.

CURRIED LAMB koftas

Koftas

1¼ pounds (600 g) ground (minced) lamb
1 small onion, coarsely grated
2 cloves garlic, finely chopped
2 green chilis, finely chopped
2 tablespoons finely chopped fresh cilantro (coriander) + extra, to garnish
2 teaspoons garam masala
½ teaspoon salt
1 large egg, lightly beaten

Curry Sauce

2 teaspoons cumin seeds
1½ teaspoons coriander seeds
1½ teaspoons hot paprika
1 teaspoon cardamom seeds
1 teaspoon ground cinnamon
1 teaspoon garam masala
1 teaspoon ground turmeric
½ teaspoon chili powder
2 cloves
2 tablespoons vegetable oil
1 onion, finely chopped
2 cloves garlic, finely chopped
1 teaspoon finely grated fresh ginger
4 tomatoes, finely chopped
¼ cup (60 ml) water
1 cup (250 g) plain yogurt

 CARBS 12g Serves 4 • Preparation 30 minutes • Cooking 20–25 minutes Difficulty 2

Koftas

1. Combine all the kofta ingredients in a large bowl and mix well. Shape into 25–30 balls. Cover and chill until required.

Curry Sauce

1. Dry-fry the cumin, coriander, paprika, cardamom, cinnamon, garam masala, turmeric, chili, and cloves in a small frying pan over medium heat until fragrant, 1–2 minutes. Transfer to a mortar and pestle or spice grinder and chop to a powder.

2. Heat the oil in a large frying pan over medium-low heat. Add the onion, garlic, ginger, and spice mix and sauté until the onion is softened, 3–4 minutes. Add the tomatoes, water, and yogurt and bring to a boil. Add the koftas and simmer over low heat until the sauce has thickened and the koftas are cooked, 15–20 minutes. Garnish with cilantro and serve hot.

This is a hearty dish and is perfect for family meals. You can prepare it ahead of time and chill in the refrigerator until ready to bake and serve. Add a chili or two to the meat sauce if you like spicy dishes.

84

ZUCCHINI lasagna

1¹/₂ pounds (750 g) zucchini (courgettes), thinly sliced into strips lengthwise

Salt

1 tablespoon extra-virgin olive oil

2 cloves garlic, finely chopped

1 pound (500 g) ground (minced) beef

1 pound (500 g) ricotta cheese

2 large eggs

¹/₂ cup chopped fresh basil

2 cups (500 ml) tomato pasta sauce (with no added sugars)

8 ounces (250 g) mozzarella cheese, shredded

¹/₃ cup (40 g) freshly grated Parmesan cheese

 CARBS 10g

Serves 6 • Preparation 30 minutes + 1 hour to drain • Cooking 45–55 minutes • Difficulty 1

1. Put the zucchini strips into a colander and sprinkle with salt. Toss to coat. Put the colander over a bowl to catch the juice. After 15 minutes, toss again. Drain for at least an hour.

2. Heat the oil in a large frying pan over medium heat. Add the garlic and sauté until softened, 3–4 minutes. Add the meat and brown all over, about 5 minutes. Set aside.

3. Combine the ricotta, eggs, and basil in a bowl. Spread the zucchini strips out on a cotton cloth to dry. Preheat the oven to 350°F (180°C/gas 4).

4. Spread ¹/₂ cup of the pasta sauce in the bottom of a 9 x 13-inch (23 x 33-cm) lasagna dish. Combine the meat with the remaining pasta sauce. Cover the sauce with a layer of zucchini. Then cover the zucchini with about one third of the ricotta mixture, one-third of the sauce, and one-third of the mozzarella cheese. Repeat, arranging the zucchini strips in the other direction. Alternate again for the third layer. After the third layer, finish with the Parmesan cheese.

5. Bake for 35–45 minutes, until the zucchini are tender and the cheese is bubbling and golden brown. Serve hot.

GRILLED VEGGIE platter

Marinade

6	cloves garlic
1	tablespoon salt
1	tablespoon dark soy sauce
$1/3$	cup (90 ml) freshly squeezed lemon or lime juice
$1/3$	cup (90 ml) sesame oil
$1/2$	cup fresh cilantro (coriander), including the stems, chopped + extra leaves, to garnish

Vegetables

1	eggplant (aubergine), with skin, cut into $1/2$-inch (1-cm) thick slices
1	red bell pepper (capsicum), seeded and quartered
1	orange bell pepper (capsicum), seeded and quartered
1	yellow bell pepper (capsicum), seeded and quartered
1	green bell pepper (capsicum), seeded and quartered
8	button mushrooms
1	onion, quartered

 CARBS 18g Serves 4 • Preparation 15 minutes + time to sit • Cooking 10–20 minutes • Difficulty 1

Marinade

1. Place all the marinade ingredients in a food processor. Process to a fine, paste-like sauce.

Vegetables

1. Put the vegetables in a large, flat dish or pan. Pour the marinade over the top. Turn the vegetables in the marinade to coat. Let sit for at least 15 minutes, or up to 4 hours in the refrigerator.

2. Preheat a grill pan (griddle) or barbecue on high heat. Grill the vegetables in the pan or over the barbecue until softened and marked with brown lines, about 10 minutes. If you are cooking the vegetables in a grill pan you may need to do them in 2 or 3 batches.

3. Serve the vegetables hot or at room temperature, garnished with the extra cilantro.

If you liked this recipe, you will love these as well.

GRILLED VEGGIES
with mozzarella

GRILLED ZUCCHINI
with arugula pesto

HOT & SPICY
brussels sprouts

This dish is a treat for coconut lovers. It is also versatile, and can be served for breakfast, lunch, or dinner.

COCONUT SPINACH with fried eggs

2	shallots, finely chopped
2	cloves garlic, finely chopped
$1/2$	teaspoon salt
4	tablespoons (60 ml) extra-virgin olive oil
$1/2$	teaspoon yellow mustard seeds
$1/2$	teaspoon whole cumin seeds
$1/2$	teaspoon red pepper flakes
14	ounces (400 g) spinach, coarsely chopped
	Freshly squeezed juice of $1/2$ lemon
6	tablespoons unsweetened shredded (desiccated) coconut, lightly toasted
6	large eggs

 CARBS 3g — Serves 4 • Preparation 15 minutes • Cooking 10 minutes • Difficulty 1

1. Combine the shallots and garlic using a mortar and pestle and sprinkle with the salt. Pound to a paste.

2. Heat 2 tablespoons of the oil in a large frying pan over medium heat. Add the mustard and cumin seeds, cover, and let toast, 1–2 minutes. Uncover and stir in the red pepper flakes. Cook for 1 minute. Stir in the garlic paste and spinach. Keep stirring until the spinach begins to wilt and is bright green, 1–2 minutes. Drizzle with the lemon juice and sprinkle with the coconut.

3. Meanwhile, heat the remaining 2 tablespoons of oil in a large frying pan and fry the eggs until done to your liking.

4. Serve the coconut spinach hot with the eggs.

If you liked this recipe, you will love these as well.

EGG curry

BASIL frittata

SPINACH & PINE NUT bake

ROAST TOMATOES & eggs

3g Serves 4 • Preparation 10 minutes • Cooking 15–20 minutes • Difficulty 1

4	medium-large ripe tomatoes	6	tablespoons freshly grated Parmesan cheese
	Salt and freshly ground black pepper	2	tablespoons extra-virgin olive oil
4	leaves basil, torn		
4	large eggs		

1. Preheat the oven to 400°F (200°C/gas 6). Oil a baking dish just large enough to hold the tomatoes in a single layer.

2. Cut the tops off the tomatoes and use a teaspoon to hollow out the centers. Place the flesh in a bowl with the basil. Season the insides of the tomatoes lightly with salt. Break an egg into each tomato and top up with the tomato and basil mixture. Season with salt and pepper and sprinkle with the cheese. Drizzle with the oil.

3. Bake for 15–20 minutes, until the tomatoes have softened and the eggs have set. Serve hot or at room temperature.

EGG curry

9g Serves 2 • Preparation 20 minutes • Cooking 20–25 minutes • Difficulty 1

1	tablespoon ghee (clarified butter) or vegetable oil	1/2	teaspoon ground chili powder
1	onion, finely chopped	1	cup (250 g) chopped tomatoes
1	(1/2-inch/1-cm) piece fresh ginger, thinly sliced	1	small bunch fresh cilantro (coriander), finely chopped
1	clove garlic, thinly sliced	4	hard-boiled eggs, peeled and left whole
1	teaspoon garam masala		
1	teaspoon coriander seeds		

1. Heat the ghee in a large frying pan over medium heat. Add the onion and sauté until golden brown, about 10 minutes.

2. Add the ginger, garlic, garam masala, coriander seeds, and ground chili and sauté for 2 minutes. Stir in the tomatoes and cook for 5 minutes.

3. Stir in the cilantro followed by the eggs. Simmer over low heat until the sauce thickens, 5 minutes. Serve hot.

TOFU burgers

4g Serves 4 • Preparation 15 minutes • Cooking 10–15 minutes • Difficulty 1

4	tablespoons (60 ml) vegetable oil	8	ounces (250 g) firm tofu, crumbled
1	small onion, chopped	1/4	cup (30 g) finely ground almonds
2	cloves garlic, chopped	2	tablespoons each sunflower seeds and sesame seeds
2	tablespoons soy sauce	2	tablespoons finely chopped parsley
1	tablespoon lemon juice		Salt and freshly ground black pepper
1/2	teaspoon ground cumin		

1. Heat 1 tablespoon of oil in a frying pan over medium heat. Add the onion and garlic and sauté until softened, 3–4 minutes. Add the soy sauce, lemon juice, and cumin and stir for 1 minute. Place in a bowl.

2. Add the tofu, almonds, sunflower seeds, sesame seeds, and parsley to the bowl. Season with salt and pepper. Shape into eight burgers.

3. Heat the remaining oil in a large frying pan. Cook the burgers until golden, 8–10 minutes. Serve hot.

ZUCCHINI frittata

5g Serves 4 • Preparation 15 minutes • Cooking 20–25 minutes • Difficulty 1

3	tablespoons extra-virgin olive oil	6	large eggs
1	clove garlic, finely chopped	1/2	cup (60 g) freshly grated pecorino or Parmesan cheese
2	pounds (1 kg) zucchini (courgettes), thinly sliced horizontally		Fresh salad greens, to serve
	Salt and freshly ground black pepper		

1. Heat the oil in a large frying pan over medium heat. Add the garlic and sauté until pale gold, about 3 minutes. Add the zucchini and sauté until tender, 5–7 minutes. Season with salt and pepper.

2. Beat the eggs and cheese in a medium bowl. Pour the egg mixture into the pan and cook until the egg is almost solid, 7–8 minutes.

3. Slide the frittata onto a plate, flip it onto another plate, and then slide it back into the pan. Cook until golden brown and the egg is cooked through, 3–4 minutes. Serve hot.

GRILLED VEGGIES with mozzarella

2   zucchini (courgettes), thickly sliced

1   long, slender eggplant (aubergine), thickly sliced

8   baby mozzarella cheeses (bocconcini), cut in half

16   cherry tomatoes

Fresh basil leaves

Salt and freshly ground black pepper

1/2 cup (120 ml) extra-virgin olive oil

 CARBS 4g

Serves 4 • Preparation 15 minutes • Cooking 15–20 minutes Difficulty 1

1. Preheat a grill pan (griddle) or barbecue over high heat.

2. Arrange the zucchini and eggplant on the grill and cook, turning often, until tender, 7–10 minutes.

3. Thread the vegetables onto metal skewers, alternating with the mozzarella, tomatoes, and basil leaves. Season with salt and pepper, and brush with the oil.

4. Cook on the grill until the cheese and tomatoes are heated through, about 5 minutes. Serve hot.

GRILLED ZUCCHINI with arugula pesto

4   zucchini (courgettes), thinly sliced lengthwise

8   tablespoons (120 ml) extra-virgin olive oil

2   tablespoons cider vinegar

1   tablespoon balsamic vinegar

1   clove garlic, thinly sliced

    Salt and freshly ground black pepper

2   cups (100 g) arugula (rocket)

6   tablespoons pine nuts

1–2   tablespoons raisins

CARBS 9g

Serves 4 • Preparation 25 minutes + 1 hour to marinate • Cooking 30 minutes • Difficulty 1

1. Place the zucchini in a small, shallow dish. Mix 3 tablespoons of oil, cider vinegar, balsamic vinegar, and garlic in a small bowl. Season with salt and pepper. Pour over the zucchini. Let marinate for 1 hour.

2. Put 1½ cups (75 g) of arugula in a blender with 4 tablespoons of pine nuts and the remaining oil and process until smooth. Drain the zucchini, reserving the marinade.

3. Preheat a grill pan (griddle) or barbecue over high heat. Grill the zucchini in batches, turning often until tender, 4–5 minutes each batch.

4. Arrange the remaining arugula on four serving plates and put the zucchini on top. Sprinkle with the remaining pine nuts and the raisins. Season with salt and pepper, and drizzle with the reserved marinade. Serve hot.

Cabbage is part of the cruciferous family of vegetables, which also includes brussels sprouts, broccoli, kale, and cauliflower. It is an excellent source of many nutrients, such as folic acid, vitamin C, and vitamin B6. Furthermore, many scientists believe that all members of the cruciferous family contain potent anticancer compounds so they recommend that we eat them regularly.

CABBAGE & COCONUT stir-fry

3	tablespoons freshly squeezed lime juice
2	tablespoons Thai fish sauce
1	teaspoon red pepper flakes or two small chilis, crumbled
3	tablespoons peanut oil
3	cups (150 g) finely shredded red cabbage
3	cups (150 g) finely shredded green or white cabbage
6	scallions (spring onions), sliced
3	cloves garlic, finely chopped
1/3	cup (40 g) unsweetened flaked coconut
1/3	cup (40 g) dry-roasted peanuts

CARBS 5g Serves 4 • Preparation 15 minutes • Cooking 5 minutes • Difficulty 1

1. Mix the lime juice, fish sauce, and red pepper flakes in a bowl and set aside.

2. Heat the oil in a large wok over medium-high heat. Add both types of cabbage, the scallions, and garlic and stir-fry until the cabbage is just wilted but still crisp, 3–4 minutes. Add the lime juice mixture and stir-fry for 1 minute. Stir in the coconut.

3. Serve hot sprinkled with the peanuts.

If you liked this recipe, you will love these as well.

CRESS & FENNEL
miso

GRILLED VEGGIE
platter

COCONUT SPINACH
with fried eggs

FRIED TOFU with mushrooms

Vegetable oil, for frying
2   pounds (1 kg) firm tofu, cubed
3   tablespoons peanut oil
2   scallions (spring onions),
    thinly sliced
1   tablespoon finely chopped
    fresh ginger
1   pound (500 g) button
    mushrooms, sliced
½   cup (125 g) thinly sliced
    bamboo shoots
1   cup (250 ml) vegetable stock
2½ tablespoons soy sauce
1   teaspoon Asian sesame oil
    Freshly ground black pepper
4   baby bok choy, cut in half
2   teaspoons cornstarch
    (cornflour)
1   tablespoon water

CARBS
3g

Serves 6 • Preparation 20 minutes • Cooking 25–30 minutes
Difficulty 1

1. Place a wok over high heat. Pour in about 2 inches (5 cm) of oil. Test the oil temperature by dropping in a small piece of bread. If it immediately bubbles to the surface and begins to turn golden, the oil is ready. Add the tofu in two batches and fry until golden brown all over, 5–7 minutes per batch. Drain on paper towels.

2. Heat the peanut oil in the wok, add the scallions and ginger and stir-fry until softened, 2–3 minutes. Add the mushrooms and stir-fry for 3 minutes. Stir in the bamboo shoots, vegetable stock, soy sauce, sesame oil, and the fried tofu. Season with pepper. Bring to a boil and simmer for 3 minutes.

3. Add the bok choy and cook for 2 minutes more. Mix the cornstarch and water in a small bowl. Stir into the wok and cook to thicken the mixture, 1–2 minutes. Serve hot.

SWEET & SPICY tofu

2 tablespoons Asian sesame oil

2 pounds (1 kg) firm tofu, cut into small cubes

2 scallions (spring onions), finely chopped

2 cloves garlic, finely chopped

1 teaspoon finely chopped fresh ginger

2 small fresh red chilis, seeded and finely chopped

1 tablespoon dry sherry

1½ tablespoons soy sauce

1 cup (250 ml) + 1 tablespoon water

½ teaspoon salt

1½ teaspoons cornstarch (cornflour)

 CARBS 3g • Serves 6 • Preparation 20 minutes • Cooking 10 minutes • Difficulty 1

1. Heat the oil in a large wok or frying pan over medium-high heat. Add the tofu, half the scallions, half the garlic, and the ginger and stir-fry for 3 minutes. Add the chilis and stir-fry for 1 minute. Stir in the sherry, soy sauce, 1 cup (250 ml) of water, and salt. Bring to a boil and simmer for 3 minutes.

2. Mix the remaining 1 tablespoon of water and cornstarch in a small bowl. Stir into the wok and cook until the mixture thickens, 2–3 minutes. Sprinkle with the remaining scallions and garlic. Transfer to a heated plate and serve hot.

Brussels sprouts are an excellent source of vitamins C and K, folic acid, and beta-carotene. Like cabbage and broccoli, they are believed to contain cancer-fighting phytochemicals.

HOT & SPICY brussels sprouts

4   tablespoons (60 ml) extra-virgin olive oil

1   pound (500 g) brussels sprouts, tough outer leaves discarded

4   cloves garlic, finely chopped

2   small dried chilis, crumbled

    Salt

2   tablespoons finely chopped fresh parsley

 CARBS 5g   Serves 4 • Preparation 15 minutes • Cooking 8–11 minutes. Difficulty 1

1. Heat the oil in a large frying pan or wok over medium-high heat. Add the brussels sprouts and stir-fry until tender and well browned. This will take 7–10 minutes.

2. Add the garlic, chilis, salt, and parsley and stir-fry for 1–2 more minutes. Serve hot.

If you liked this recipe, you will love these as well.

COCONUT SPINACH
with fried eggs

CABBAGE & COCONUT
stir-fry

SPINACH & PINE NUT
bake

BASIL frittata

12 large eggs

1 cup (120 g) freshly grated pecorino or Parmesan cheese

Salt and freshly ground black pepper

Bunch of fresh basil, coarsely chopped + extra leaves, to garnish

2 tablespoons extra-virgin olive oil

CARBS 0g · Serves 6 • Preparation 10 minutes • Cooking 6–10 minutes
Difficulty 2

1. Beat the eggs in a large bowl. Add the cheese and season with salt and pepper. Add the basil and mix well.

2. Heat the oil in a large frying pan over medium heat. Pour the egg mixture into the pan and cook until the bottom is browned, 3–5 minutes.

3. Slide the frittata onto a plate, flip it onto another plate, and then slide it back into the pan. Cook until the egg is cooked through and lightly browned all over, 3–4 minutes. Garnish with the extra basil and serve hot.

MUSHROOM & RICOTTA *frittata*

2   tablespoons extra-virgin olive oil

1   small onion, finely sliced

2   cloves garlic, finely chopped

8   ounces (250 g) brown or cremini mushrooms, sliced

8   large eggs, lightly beaten

1/4   cup (60 g) fresh ricotta cheese, drained

1/4   cup (40 g) shaved ricotta salata or Parmesan cheese

2   tablespoons finely chopped fresh oregano

    Salt and freshly ground black pepper

CARBS
2g

Serves 4 • Preparation 15 minutes • Cooking 15–20 minutes
Difficulty 1

1. Preheat an overhead broiler (grill) to medium-high heat. Heat the oil in a medium ovenproof frying pan over medium-low heat. Add the onion and garlic and sauté until softened, 3–4 minutes. Add the mushrooms and sauté until golden brown, 6–8 minutes.

2. Spread the mushroom mixture evenly in the pan and pour in the eggs. Sprinkle the ricotta, ricotta salata, and oregano over the top. Season with salt and pepper and cook over medium-low heat until almost set, about 5 minutes.

3. Place the pan under the broiler and cook until the cheese has melted and frittata is completely set, about 2 minutes. Slice into portions and serve hot or at room temperature.

Spinach is packed with vitamins and minerals, including vitamins C and K, folic acid, iron, and magnesium. It contains good quantities of lutein, which is believed to promote healthy eyesight, among other things.

SPINACH & PINE NUT bake

1   pound (500 g) spinach
4   large eggs, separated
$^1/_2$ cup (60 g) freshly grated Parmesan cheese
      Freshly ground black pepper
$^1/_4$ cup (30 g) pine nuts, toasted

 CARBS 2g

Serves 4 • Preparation 15 minutes • Cooking 8–12 minutes
Difficulty 1

1. Preheat the oven to 425°F (220°C/gas 7).

2. Cook the spinach in a pot of lightly salted water until tender, 3–4 minutes. Drain well and chop in a food processor until smooth.

3. Beat the egg whites in a large bowl with an electric mixer on medium speed until stiff.

4. Mix the egg yolks with the spinach in a separate bowl until well combined. Stir in the Parmesan. Season with pepper. Carefully fold the egg whites into the spinach mixture.

5. Spoon the mixture into a small ovenproof pan and sprinkle with the pine nuts. Bake for 5–7 minutes, until risen and the pine nuts are golden brown. Serve hot.

If you liked this recipe, you will love these as well.

COCONUT SPINACH
with fried eggs

BASIL
frittata

MUSHROOM & RICOTTA
frittata

This is a delicious stew, packed with nourishing vegetables. Vary the amount of chili powder and sauce according to your personal tastes.

SPICY VEGETABLE stew

2	tablespoons peanut oil
1	teaspoon cumin seeds
1	onion, thinly sliced
2	stalks celery, chopped
2	cloves garlic, sliced
1	teaspoon green curry paste
1	red bell pepper (capsicum), seeded and sliced
2	zucchini (courgettes), sliced
1	medium eggplant (aubergine), chopped
8	ounces (250 g) button mushrooms, quartered
2	(14-ounce/400-g) cans tomatoes, with juice
1	tablespoon Thai sweet chili sauce
1	teaspoon chili powder
2	teaspoons ground coriander
1	cup (200 g) canned red kidney beans, drained
	Freshly squeezed juice of 1 lemon
2	tablespoons coarsely chopped fresh cilantro (coriander)

 CARBS 18g Serves 4 • Preparation 20 minutes • Cooking 35 minutes. • Difficulty 1

1. Heat the oil in a large saucepan over medium heat. Add the cumin seeds and sauté until fragrant, about 2 minutes. Add the onion, celery, garlic, and curry paste and cook until the onions are softened, about 5 minutes.

2. Add the bell pepper, zucchini, eggplant, mushrooms, and tomatoes. Cover and simmer over medium heat until the vegetables begin to soften, about 5 minutes. Add the chili sauce, chili powder, and coriander. Mix well, then add the kidney beans. Cover and simmer until the vegetables are tender, about 20 minutes, stirring occasionally.

3. Stir in the lemon juice and cilantro. Serve hot.

If you liked this recipe, you will love these as well.

GRILLED VEGGIE platter

CABBAGE & COCONUT stir-fry

HOT & SPICY brussels sprouts

MOCHA cheesecake

Cheesecake

5	large eggs, at room temperature
½	cup (120 ml) strongly brewed black coffee, warm
¼	cup (30 g) unsweetened cocoa powder
2	pounds (1 kg) cream cheese, softened
1	cup (24 packets) sugar substitute, such as Splenda

Mocha Ganache

¼	cup (60 ml) heavy (double) cream
3	tablespoons unsweetened cocoa powder

Whipped cream, to serve
Coffee powder, to serve

 CARBS 2g Serves 12 • Preparation 30 minutes + 7 hours to cool & chill
Cooking: 60–70 minutes • Difficulty 2

Cheesecake

1. Crack the eggs into a small bowl and set aside. Mix the coffee and cocoa in a small bowl until smooth and set aside. Preheat the oven to 350°F (180°C/gas 4). Grease a 12-inch (30-cm) springform pan.

2. Beat the cream cheese with an electric mixer until smooth. Add the sugar substitute and beat until well mixed. With the mixer on low, add half of the coffee and chocolate mixture. Add the eggs gradually, beating until just combined after each addition. Pour the mixture into the prepared pan. Bake for 60–70 minutes, until set in the middle. Cool for an hour.

Mocha Ganache

1. Put the cream in a small saucepan over low heat and bring to a gentle simmer. Remove from the heat and stir in the cocoa. Return to low heat and continue stirring until smooth and thickened.

2. Stir in the remaining coffee mixture. Simmer for 1 minute then remove from the heat. Let cool, then pour over the cooled cheesecake.

3. Chill for at least 6 hours. Decorate with the whipped cream and coffee powder just before serving.

We made this recipe using the sugar substitute known as Splenda, which contains only a fraction of the sugar and carbohydrates found in sugar. The sweetening agent it contains is called sucralose and, unlike many artifical sweeteners, it can be used for baking.
Vital wheat gluten, also known as gluten flour, is a powdered form of gluten. It adds chewiness to baked goods, which can be lacking when wheat flour is not included in the ingredients.

CITRUS pound cake

1³/₄	cups (270 g) almond flour
¹/₄	cup (30 g) vital wheat gluten (gluten flour)
1	teaspoon baking powder
¹/₂	teaspoon salt
³/₄	cup (180 g) unsalted butter, softened
2	ounces (60 g) cream cheese, softened
5	large eggs, at room temperature
1¹/₂	cups (32 packets) sugar substitute, such as Splenda
1	tablespoon finely grated unwaxed lemon zest
1	tablespoon finely grated unwaxed orange zest

CARBS 3g

Serves 12 • Preparation 15 minutes • Cooking 50–55 minutes
Difficulty 1

1. Preheat the oven to 325°F (170°C/gas 3). Butter a 10-inch (25-cm) tube cake pan. Combine the almond flour, vital wheat gluten, baking powder, and salt in a bowl.

2. Beat the butter, cream cheese, and sugar substitute in a large bowl with an electric mixer on medium speed until pale and creamy. Add the eggs, one at a time, beating until just combined after each addition. With the mixer on low speed, gradually beat in the flour mixture and lemon and orange zests.

3. Spoon into the prepared pan. Bake for 50–55 minutes, until risen and golden brown. Let cool in the pan for 15 minutes, then remove the pan sides and base and lt cool completely on a wire rack.

If you liked this recipe, you will love these as well.

BANANA SPICE cake

LEMON CREAM
with citrus salad

ALMOND cookies

CHANPAGNE strawberries

CARBS 11g · Serves 4 • Preparation 10 minutes + 2 hours to chill • Difficulty 1

| 3 | cups (450 g) strawberries, halved | 2 | cups (500 ml) chilled, very dry champagne |
| 2 | tablespoons orange-flavored liqueur | | |

1. Put the strawberries in a medium glass bowl and drizzle with the orange-flavored liqueur. Pour 1 cup (250 ml) of champagne into the bowl. Cover and chill in the refrigerator for 2 hours.

2. Divide the strawberries and their juices evenly among four serving glasses. Pour the remaining champagne over the top and serve.

BERRY FRUIT salad

CARBS 15g · Serves 6 • Preparation 10 minutes + 2–3 hours to cool & chill • Cooking 1–2 minutes • Difficulty 1

1¼	cups (300 ml) dry white wine	2	cups (300 g) raspberries
2	tablespoons superfine (caster) sugar	1	cup (150 g) blackberries
1	teaspoon finely grated unwaxed lemon zest	1	cup (150 g) blackcurrants
1	clove		
2	cups (300 g) strawberries, sliced		

1. Combine the wine, sugar, lemon zest, and clove in a small saucepan. Bring to a boil, then simmer until the sugar is dissolved, 1–2 minutes. Remove from the heat and let cool a little.

2. Combine the strawberries, raspberries, blackberries, and blackcurrants in a serving bowl. Pour the warm syrup over the top. Let cool to room temperature, about 1 hour.

3. Chill in the refrigerator for 1–2 hours. Remove the clove before serving.

BAKED ricotta

CARBS 23g · Serves 4 • Preparation 10 minutes • Cooking 40 minutes • Difficulty 1

2	cups (500 g) fresh ricotta cheese, drained	2	tablespoons (30 ml) brandy
4	tablespoons (50 g) orange marmalade	2	tablespoons all-purpose (plain) flour
2	large eggs, lightly beaten		

1. Preheat the oven to 325°F (170°C/gas 3). Mix the ricotta, marmalade, eggs, brandy, and flour in a large bowl. Spoon the mixture evenly into 1-cup (250-ml) ramekins.

2. Bake for 40 minutes. Turn off the oven and leave the door ajar until the ricotta is completely cool.

3. Serve at room temperature.

MELON & CILANTRO salad

CARBS 10g · Serves 4 • Preparation 15 minutes + 2 hours to chill • Difficulty 1

1½	cups (250 g) cubed cantaloupe (rock) melon	3	tablespoons coarsely chopped cilantro (coriander)
1½	cups (250 g) cubed honeydew melon	¼	cup (40 g) flaked almonds, toasted
1½	cups (250 g) cubed watermelon		

1. Combine the melons in a large bowl. Add the cilantro and almonds. Toss gently but well.

2. Chill for 2 hours before serving.

MANGO cream

1   ripe mango, peeled, and coarsely chopped
1   tablespoon freshly squeezed lemon juice
1   tablespoon freshly squeezed lime juice
1–3 tablespoons freshly squeezed orange juice
1   cup (250 g) mascarpone cheese
1   cup (250 g) heavy (double) cream
2   tablespoons sugar substitute, such as Splenda

 Serves 6 • Preparation 15 minutes + 2–3 hours to chill • Difficulty 1

1. Combine the mango, lemon juice, lime juice, and 1 tablespoon of the orange juice in a blender and purée until smooth. If it is too stiff, add more orange juice. Press through a fine-mesh sieve into a bowl. Refrigerate until chilled, about 1 hour.

2. Whip the mascarpone with an electric mixer at low speed until smooth. Stir into the mango mixture. Beat the cream with the sugar substitute in another bowl until thick. Fold into the mango mixture. Spoon into six dessert glasses. Chill for 2–3 hours before serving.

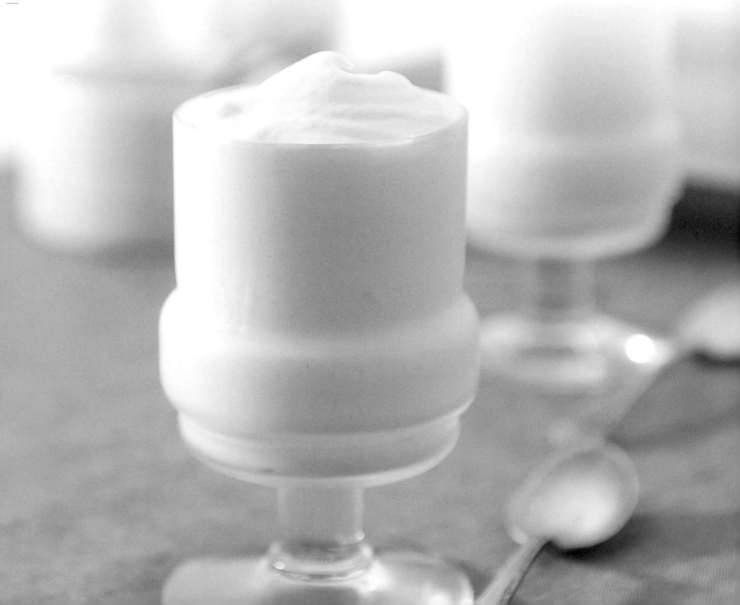

STRAWBERRY YOGURT *sorbet*

½ cup (12 packets) sugar substitute, such as Splenda

2 cups (500 ml) water

3 cups (450 g) ripe strawberries, chopped

1¼ cups (300 g) plain yogurt

 15g

Serves 4 • Preparation 15 minutes + 30 minutes to cool + time to churn • Cooking 2–3 minutes • Difficulty 1

1. Place the sugar substitute and water in a medium saucepan over medium heat. Bring to a boil and simmer, stirring constantly, until the sugar substitute has completely dissolved, 2–3 minutes. Remove from the heat and set aside to cool, about 30 minutes.

2. Add the strawberries to the cooled syrup. Stir in the yogurt then chop the mixture in a food processor until smooth. Transfer to an ice-cream machine and freeze according to the manufacturer's instructions.

3. Transfer to a freezer-proof container and freeze until ready to serve.

Following a low-carb diet usually means cutting out most sweet treats and desserts. But there are some dishes that can be served without doing too much harm; serve small portions and on special occasions. Erythritol is a naturally derived sugar substitute which contains almost no calories and has a zero glycemic index.

114

BANANA SPICE cake

2	cups (300 g) almond flour
1	teaspoon baking powder
1	teaspoon ground cinnamon
1/8	teaspoon ground cloves
1/2	cup (120 g) salted butter, softened
4	ounces (120 g) cream cheese, softened
1	cup (24 packets) sugar substitute, such as Splenda
1/2	cup erythritol
5	large eggs, at room temperature
2	teaspoons banana extract (essence)
1	teaspoon vanilla extract (essence)

CARBS **6g**

Serves 8 • Preparation 15 minutes • Cooking 50–55 minutes
Difficulty 1

1. Preheat the oven to 350°F (180°C/gas 4). Lightly grease a 9-inch (23-cm) springform pan. Combine the almond flour, baking powder, cinnamon, and cloves in a bowl.

2. Beat the butter, cream cheese, sugar substitute, and erythritol in a large bowl with an electric mixer on medium speed until pale and creamy. Add the eggs, one at a time, beating until just combined after each addition. With the mixer on low speed, gradually beat in the almond mixture, and banana and vanilla extracts.

3. Spoon the batter into the prepared pan. Bake for 50–55 minutes, until risen and golden brown. Let cool in the pan for 15 minutes, then turn out onto a rack and let cool completely.

If you liked this recipe, you will love these as well.

MOCHA cheesecake

CITRUS pound cake

ALMOND cookies

LEMON CREAM with citrus salad

Lemon Cream

2	cups (500 ml) heavy (double) cream
1/2	cup (12 packets) sugar substitute, such as Splenda
1/3	cup (90 ml) freshly squeezed lemon juice
2	tablespoons water
2	teaspoons unflavored gelatin powder

Citrus Salad

	Freshly squeezed juice of 1 lemon
1	blood orange, peeled and segmented
1	orange, peeled and segmented
2	tangerines (mandarins), peeled and segmented
1	lime, peeled and segmented

 CARBS 5g • Serves 6 • Preparation 25 minutes + 12 hours to chill • Cooking 10 minutes • Difficulty 1

Lemon Cream

1. Heat the cream and sugar substitute in a small saucepan over medium heat until well mixed. Bring to a boil and simmer for 5 minutes. Remove from the heat.

2. Put the lemon juice and water in a small saucepan. Sprinkle with the gelatin and set aside for 5 minutes. Gently warm over low heat, stirring until the gelatin has melted. Remove from the heat and let cool before adding to the cream mixture. Strain the lemon cream through a fine-mesh sieve into a bowl. Pour evenly into six dessert glasses. Place the glasses on a tray and chill in the refrigerator overnight.

Citrus Salad

1. Combine the lemon juice, blood orange, orange, tangerines, and lime segments in a bowl and toss well to coat. Chill in the refrigerator for 30 minutes.

2. Top each glass of lemon cream with citrus salad and serve.

BAKED nutmeg custard

2¹/₂ cups (625 ml) milk

3 large eggs + 1 large egg yolk

¹/₃ cup (9 packets) sugar substitute, such as Splenda

1¹/₂ teaspoons vanilla extract (essence)

¹/₂ teaspoon ground nutmeg

1. Preheat the oven to 300°F (150°C/gas 2). Oil four 1-cup (250-ml) ramekins. Place the milk in a medium saucepan over medium heat and bring to a boil. Remove from the heat and set aside.

2. Whisk the eggs, egg yolk, sugar, and vanilla in a medium bowl until just combined. Gradually pour the hot milk into the egg mixture, stirring with a wooden spoon until incorporated. Strain the custard mixture through a fine-mesh sieve into a small bowl or pitcher (jug).

3. Place the ramekins in a deep baking pan. Pour the custard mixture into the ramekins and dust with the nutmeg. Pour enough boiling water into the baking pan to come halfway up the sides of the ramekins. Bake for 30 minutes, until set but still a little wobbly in the center. Serve at room temperature or chilled.

Almonds are relatively low in carbohydrates and they are very low in cholesterol and sodium. They are a very good source of Vitamin E, and regular consumption is believed to help lower cholesterol. Each cookie contains 2 grams of carbohydrates.

ALMOND cookies

2	cups (300 g) almond flour
1/2	cup (12 packets) sugar substitute, such as Splenda
1/2	cup (120 g) unsalted butter, softened
1/2	teaspoon salt
1	teaspoon vanilla extract (essence)
1/2	teaspoon almond extract (essence)

 CARBS 2g Makes 16 • Preparation 10 minutes • Cooking 20 minutes. Difficulty 1

1. Preheat the oven to 300°F (150°C/gas 2). Butter a large baking sheet. Line with parchment paper.

2. Combine all the ingredients in a large bowl, stirring until well mixed. Shape the dough into walnut-size balls and place on the prepared baking sheet, spacing well.

3. Bake for 5 minutes. Press down lightly with a fork, then bake for 15 more minutes, until golden brown. Let cool on the sheet for 2–3 minutes, then transfer to a wire rack and let cool completely.

If you liked this recipe, you will love these as well.

ALMOND pancakes

CITRUS pound cake

BANANA SPICE cake